THREE MEN ON A HORSE

★

A COMEDY IN THREE ACTS

BY JOHN CECIL HOLM AND GEORGE ABBOTT

★

DRAMATISTS
PLAY SERVICE
INC.

Three Men on a Horse was first produced by Alex Yokel at The Playhouse in New York City on January 30, 1935. The play was staged by Mr. Abbott, the settings were designed by Boris Aronson, and the cast was as follows:

AUDREY TROWBRIDGE	Joyce Arling
THE TAILOR	J. Ascher Smith
ERWIN TROWBRIDGE	William Lynn
CLARENCE DOBBINS	Fleming Ward
DELIVERY BOY	Nick Wiger
HARRY	James Lane
CHARLIE	Millard Mitchell
FRANKIE	Teddy Hart
PATSY	Sam Levene
MABEL	Shirley Booth
MOSES	Richard Huey
GLORIA	Edith Van Cleve
AL	Garson Kanin
HOTEL MAID	Margaret Mullen
MR. CARVER	Frank Camp

NOTE. The present text includes a few music cues. These follow the professional production, but the music is not necessary. Special arrangements must be made, in case the music is used, with the original publishers.

SCENES

ACT I

SCENE 1. The living room of the Trowbridge house, Ozone Heights, New Jersey.

SCENE 2. A barroom in the basement of the Lavillere Hotel, New York City.

ACT II

SCENE 1. Ozone Heights.

SCENE 2. A room in the Lavillere Hotel.

ACT III

SCENE 1. Ozone Heights.

SCENE 2. The hotel room.

THREE MEN ON A HORSE

ACT I

SCENE 1: *The living room of the Trowbridge home, Ozone Heights, New Jersey. A typical standardized house. There is a stairway leading up, a door to kitchen and a front door. See diagrams at end of book.*
Orchestra plays "My Little Gray Home in the West."
AT RISE: AUDREY *enters from kitchen carrying a plate of toast which she places on table. It is a bridge table. Already on table are coffee, orange juice and toast.* AUDREY *is about 25. Wears house dress. As she crosses to foot of stairs she examines sole of one of her bedroom slippers.*

AUDREY. (*Calling.*) Erwin.
ERWIN. (*Off.*) Yes.
AUDREY. The paint you put on the kitchen floor isn't dry yet.
ERWIN. Well, I didn't expect it would be. It says on the can it takes forty-eight hours.
AUDREY. Oh. Anyway I set up the bridge table in the living room. Breakfast is all ready.
ERWIN. All right.

(AUDREY *fills coffee cups from percolator. While doing this door buzzer rings. She sets percolator on table, goes up and opens door and admits the* TAILOR.)

AUDREY. Oh, yes. Just a minute. (*Calls.*) Erwin.
ERWIN. (*Off.*) Yes.
AUDREY. (*At foot of stairs.*) The man is here for your suit. Will you bring it down?
ERWIN. All right. Just a second.
AUDREY. (*Over her shoulder to* TAILOR *who is standing right in back of her at door.*) Just a second!
ERWIN. (*Pause.*) Here it comes.

(*Suit lands at* AUDREY'S *feet. While* AUDREY *cleans out pockets of handkerchief, pipe, matches, etc., she speaks.*)

AUDREY. The last time I sent this suit I forgot to take out a white handkerchief with a blue border and it never came back.

TAILOR. I'll tell him about it.

AUDREY. (*Finds little address book in pocket. Pats pockets to be sure she has everything, then hands him suit.*) It was a good handkerchief. (TAILOR *exits.* AUDREY *places contents of suit on table then curious about book she picks it up and looks through it — is shocked and distressed — looks up stairs — goes to phone cautiously. Picks up phone.*) Give me 42 W — Ring 4. (*Sits*) Hello, Clarence. . . . (*Weakly.*) I wonder if you could come over for a minute. I just found something that's upset me. . . . You will. . . . Oh, thanks. (*Hangs up. Wipes tear away, blows nose, then calls*) Erwin, breakfast is ready.

ERWIN. (*Upstairs.*) All right, dear. (AUDREY *crosses to table, sits, blows nose and looks straight ahead.* ERWIN *comes down from stairs and into room. He is dressed, except for his necktie. He places one foot on chair* R. *and ties a shoe lace.*) I thought of another verse while I was shaving. Darned good, too —— (*Sits at table.*) What's the matter, dear, something get in your eye?

AUDREY. I'll be all right.

ERWIN. Gee, that's too bad. It's this dry spell we're having. Dust everywhere.

AUDREY. Better drink your coffee before it's too cold.

ERWIN. Oh, yes. (*Starts eating.*)

AUDREY. You forgot your necktie.

ERWIN. (*Looks.*) Necktie? So I have. Oh, I couldn't decide which tie to wear.

AUDREY. You need some new ones, I guess.

ERWIN. No, no. I have plenty. Gee I'm late —— (*Looks at wrist watch.*)

AUDREY. (*Suddenly; crossing to table.*) You told me you'd stay home from the office one day this week.

ERWIN. I know I did, sweetheart — but not today. How in Heaven's name am I going to turn out sixty-seven Mother's Day greetings?

AUDREY. (*Suddenly; hopefully.*) You could write them in the country. We could go for a drive. (*Sits at table* L.)

ERWIN. No. No. I know I couldn't. I've never been able to write in the country — the birds and the butterflies distract me —— (*Sud-*

iently.) Wait —— (*He holds up finger.*) "The birds and the butterflies send you a greeting. It's spring and today in mem'ry we're meeting." Mother's Day Number Eleven. Yes, that's all right — well, that's another one. I'll call that "To Mother on Mother's Day" —— (*Takes out pencil and writes on envelope; then starts gulping breakfast. She goes to window* R.) What's the matter?

AUDREY. I'm expecting Clarence, that's all.

ERWIN. I wish you'd have him visit when I'm not here; he gets me upset — he laughs at me — calls me the Poet of Dobbins Drive.

AUDREY. He doesn't understand. He's a business man.

ERWIN. Business man? Every time I look out the window, I see forty-six empty houses that he's built and can't sell. My greeting card verses are read from Asbury Park to Seattle, Washington.

AUDREY. Well, I'm not going to be happy in Ozone Heights — after today.

ERWIN. (*Turning around in his chair to look at her.*) Why, has something happened?

AUDREY. Yes — something has. Erwin ——

ERWIN. I wish you wouldn't say Erwin in that tone of voice, Audrey. I know my name is Erwin, but it makes me feel whatever has happened has something to do with me.

AUDREY. It has.

ERWIN. Why, Audrey ——

AUDREY. I discovered it before you came down.

ERWIN. About me? Why — why, what is it?

AUDREY. I'm going to wait until brother gets here.

ERWIN. (*Looks at watch.*) Do you have to have him here to tell me what it is?

AUDREY. Yes. . . . Erwin, you don't love me any more. (*Sits on davenport, bursts into tears.*)

ERWIN. (*Crossing to her.*) Why, Audrey, of course I love you. Maybe I don't walk up and say, "Audrey, I love you," every time I see you . . . (*Sits and put arm around her.*) but you know how I feel. Gosh, I don't know how other husbands act. But I always do the best I can and we seem to get along all right. If I've done anything that's wrong I'd rather have you tell me than tell your brother. (*Turns front.*) I wish you wouldn't start the day off like this. It's hard to write my verses if I'm in the wrong mood, you know that. Come on, dear, tell Erwin what it is so he can explain and get to the office. . . .

AUDREY. Well, this morning the man came for your blue suit — and I gave it to him.

ERWIN. Well . . . why are we so excited about it? You were the one who said it needed cleaning.

(CLARENCE *enters. He is about 35. Small-town business man. Pen and pencils in breast pocket, lodge emblems corner of vest.*)

CLARENCE. Well, good morning. What's happened? (*He looks at tieless collar on* ERWIN.) Oh, just getting up?

AUDREY. (*Rises.*) Good morning — Clarence.

CLARENCE. (*Coming down* L.) Hello, sis — you look all upset. Has he been doing anything to you?

ERWIN. I haven't done a thing that I know of. I was just having breakfast. It's something about my suit. My blue suit. Audrey sent it out to be cleaned.

CLARENCE. You being funny?

ERWIN. Maybe you think it's funny. I don't. I should be at the office and my wife tells me I don't love her any more.

CLARENCE. What has that got to do with a blue suit?

AUDREY. I sent it out to be cleaned, an' — (*Crossing and taking notebook from pocket of dress.*) I found this notebook in the coat pocket.

ERWIN. Oh, that book. Is that what upset you . . .

AUDREY. (*Holds up hand; goes to* CLARENCE, *flips pages.*) Look at those names . . . Shirley, May, Lena Wee, Bambola, Nell Mc-Clatchy, Squeeze . . . not one or two, Clarence, but pages of them . . . look at those telephone numbers. . . . Jamaica 6-2-3-1. . . .

ERWIN. But darling!

CLARENCE. My gosh, say. What are you keeping . . . a harem?

ERWIN. Wait, dear. (*Meekly.*) I can explain. It's only a hobby.

AUDREY. Only a hobby. Oh —— (*Sits — cries.*)

ERWIN. They're horses.

CLARENCE. Horses, huh —

AUDREY. Horses!

ERWIN. Horse racing.

CLARENCE. Oh, is that it?

ERWIN. Yes!

CLARENCE. (*Crossing* R. *to* ERWIN.) I always knew you had some secret vice. I was telling Audrey just the other day . . .

ERWIN. I don't play them.

CLARENCE. Then what do you do?

ERWIN. I dope them out.

CLARENCE. For who? For what?

ERWIN. For fun. I do it on the bus on the way to the office to pass the time. Like some people do cross words . . .

CLARENCE. Oh, you do?

ERWIN. Yes — one day I came across a racing paper on the bus and I found out that the fellow who doped them out wasn't so good. So the next day I did it myself for fun . . . and I've been keeping track of them in that book.

AUDREY. (*Rises.*) But Erwin, you haven't explained all these numbers.

ERWIN. (*Going to* AUDREY.) Certainly I have, sweetheart. (*Takes book.*) Listen. Here I wrote on one page Jamaica-6—that's the sixth race. And then 2-3-1. The 2, 3, and 1 was in the order I thought the entries would finish. On this other page is the way they did finish. (*Turning page.*)

CLARENCE. (*Looking at book.*) You mean you guessed them right?

ERWIN. (*Like a little boy.*) Sure.

AUDREY. But that doesn't explain this number. (*Looking at book.*) This 896.50 ——

ERWIN. It isn't a number. That's what I made the week of January 20th—at two dollars a bet. $896.50.

AUDREY. You made that and never told me?

ERWIN. Only on paper, sweetheart. Oh, I'd never bet on a horse. You know we couldn't afford that. (*To* CLARENCE.) Look—in the back of the book is what I would have made on a four horse parlay, playing two dollars a day. $14,000.50 since January first. It's what you call mental betting.

CLARENCE. (*Looking in book; busineslike.*) So you win on paper. (*Takes book.*)

ERWIN. (*Crossing, sitting at table.*) But I wouldn't bet on a horse with real money.

CLARENCE. But on paper with two dollars bets you've made a few thousand dollars. Suppose you did put two dollars on a horse? And the horse paid three to one . . . you would have six dollars beside the original two dollars you bet.

(AUDREY *sits.*)

ERWIN. Yes. But suppose the horse didn't win, I'd be out two dollars. Two dollars is a lot of money to us, Clarence.

CLARENCE. But according to your little book here, you couldn't have picked many horses that lost or you wouldn't have run up those figures.

ERWIN. Oh, yes, I have! Now last Tuesday, going to town, I went through the entries in the morning paper and picked out horses 1-2-3 in all the races and the one I picked in the fourth race fell down and finished out of the money and one lost his rider and three were scratched.

CLARENCE. How about the other horses?

ERWIN. (*Eating.*) Oh, they finished all right.

CLARENCE. 1-2-3?

ERWIN. 1-2-3.

CLARENCE. How long have you been doing this, Erwin?

ERWIN. Only since the first of the year.

CLARENCE. Well, that's long enough.

ERWIN. That isn't very long——

CLARENCE. I mean that's long enough to sock it away.

ERWIN. Sock what away?

CLARENCE. Come on now, Erwin. I've been around. I can see through you.

ERWIN. I don't know what you mean, Clarence.

CLARENCE. How many savings accounts have you, Erwin?

ERWIN. You mean banks?

CLARENCE. Yes, banks.

ERWIN. Only one. The Bowery Savings Bank.

CLARENCE. How much you got in there?

ERWIN. It's down to twenty-two dollars now.

CLARENCE. Say, Erwin, you're as plain as pie to me. You've been playing the horses since January—you've won a pile of money—you don't want anyone to know about it—so what do you do? You cry poor. So we'll think you're broke.

ERWIN. I am broke.

CLARENCE. I'll bet you've got about six different bank accounts under "non de plums."

AUDREY. Why, Erwin——

ERWIN. But I haven't, honest. I wish I had.

CLARENCE. (*Sits*) Now listen—you might die tomorrow, Erwin, and nobody knows about those bank accounts but you. Think of Audrey.

ERWIN. But honest, Clarence, I haven't any money. I don't know how you can think up things like this. Gee—if I had a brain like yours, I'd write detective stories. I only do this for fun—it's just a hobby—like—like—like golf—or—or tropical fish.

CLARENCE. Is that the truth?

ERWIN. That's the truth, Clarence!

CLARENCE. Great grief, man. Why don't you bet?

ERWIN. That would spoil it all.

CLARENCE. Do you mean to tell me you can pick horses that win every day, and be satisfied with paper profits?

ERWIN. Yes.

CLARENCE. Why?

ERWIN. Because I did bet once.

AUDREY. Why, when was that, Erwin?

ERWIN. Well, that was a long time ago. . . . I guess it doesn't harm to tell about it now. We'd only been married a little while. You wanted something and I wanted to get it for you . . . you said it was too expensive . . .

CLARENCE. What happened to the horse?

ERWIN. Oh, he lost.

AUDREY. Oh.

ERWIN. He was a good horse, though. One of the fellows at the office showed me a telegram right from the jockey who was going to ride in the race, saying, "It's a sure thing and to play right on the nose . . ." So I did. I took ten dollars out of my envelope. . . . That was the time I told you my pocket was picked—remember? I was only making thirty then ——

CLARENCE. So you thought the race was fixed, huh?

ERWIN. I didn't know anything about that. But he sure was a good horse . . . maybe something went wrong. Just as the race was about to start . . . my horse broke the barrier and ran all the way around the track before they could catch him . . . so they brought him back to the post. . . . When the race started he was so tired he just stayed there.

CLARENCE. (*Rising and crossing* L.) How do you pick these horses, Erwin?

ERWIN. When I get on the bus, I just look through the entries and pick out the ones I like. I guess you'd call it playing hunches.

CLARENCE. (*Turning back to* ERWIN.) Just for the fun of it. I guess a lot of people do that. I'll bet you even know what's going to win today.

ERWIN. Sure. I figured it out last night on the bus coming home—but I only figured the first race. "Brass Monkey" is going to win it. (*Puts book in pocket.*)

CLARENCE. "Brass Monkey" ——

ERWIN. Sure, he's a good horse.

AUDREY. (*Going to* ERWIN.) I'm awfully sorry, Erwin, I suspected you of anything wrong.

ERWIN. (*Kissing* AUDREY *on forehead.*) That's all right, darling. I'd never do anything behind your back, you know that.

CLARENCE. But great grief, Erwin, you don't seem to have any initiative. No other man would have let a chance like that slip through his fingers.—Why don't you bet?

ERWIN. I don't think it would be moral for me to bet—we haven't enough money ——

CLARENCE. That's ridiculous.—Why don't you make some? I told you I'd give you a percentage if you sold one of my houses ——

AUDREY. That's sweet of you, Clarence.

ERWIN. I don't think I could sell one. Maybe Audrey could. I don't like them. (*He goes upstage.*)

CLARENCE. What do you mean you don't like them?

ERWIN. I don't like them, that's all, and I couldn't sell anything I don't like.

AUDREY. (*Rising.*) What's wrong with them?

ERWIN. (*Turning up near door.*) There isn't anything wrong with them exactly, but—well—there is too much water in the cellar.

CLARENCE. (*Going to* ERWIN.) Now I don't want any minor criticisms from you after that porch you tacked on the house—I built a beautiful row of houses all alike, and you tacked that thing on. You put this house out of step, you know that?

ERWIN. Now listen, Clarence. (CLARENCE *turns.*) Never mind, I'm late. (*Starts to go.*)

AUDREY. Wait a minute, Erwin.

ERWIN. What's the matter, darling? I have to go to work.

AUDREY. Don't you think you better apologize to Clarence before you go?

ERWIN. Apologize? For what?

AUDREY. For being so rude.

ERWIN. Rude?

AUDREY. Yes. About the houses. Erwin!

ERWIN. Well, I apologize—but I don't like water in the cellar—I don't think it adds anything to a house. (*Buzzer.* ERWIN *opens door.*)

BOY. (*Delivery boy in uniform.*) No. 1 Dobbins Drive?

ERWIN. That's right.

BOY. Package for Mrs. Trowbridge.

ERWIN. There she is there . . . (*Starts out.*)

BOY. C. O. D. Forty-eight dollars.

ERWIN. (*Coming back.*) What?

AUDREY. I bought some dresses, darling.

ERWIN. C. O. D. Forty-eight dollars? How are we going to pay it—what made you do that?

CLARENCE. I told her she needed some decent clothes. That's why and since I've found out a few things today, I guess I was right.

ERWIN. We can't afford it —— (*To* BOY.) Take them back, son.

BOY. I can't take them back. They've been altered.

AUDREY. That's right, Erwin. It was a sale. They'd cost sixty-five next week. I saved you seventeen dollars. Darling, you know I didn't have anything to wear.

ERWIN. Nothing to wear! All I seem to do is pay for dresses and hats . . . and my life insurance. (*Crosses to bookcase, takes out "Household Budget Book." Looks through book.*)

CLARENCE. Don't yell at my sister like that.

ERWIN. Nothing to wear. (*Reads.*) Listen—1929—6 dresses—4 hats—1930—7 dresses—5 hats—1931—32 and 33—8—9—and 10 dresses and 5—4—and 8 hats respectively—altogether that's 40 dresses and 32 hats. I should be in the hat business instead of trying to get some place.

AUDREY. Darling, it does sound like a lot, I know, but that's since 1929—some of those hats I couldn't wear because my hair was growing back and they didn't fit.

ERWIN. Here's my hat—five dollars it cost me in 1931 and it's good enough for me, Fall, Winter, Spring and Summer—and look at it. (*Placing hat on his head.*)

CLARENCE. Women's things are different—some women buy ——

ERWIN. Well look at it.

AUDREY. I'm looking. I have a right to have a dress or two. I've saved a little money from the budget and anyway how do I know you haven't been betting on the horses?

CLARENCE. Yes there's a lot of things about you I'd like to know ——

ERWIN. My gosh, don't I bring home my salary every week? You know I never bet on a horse or anything.

AUDREY. (*Going to* CLARENCE.) Oh, Clarence, let's not argue any more ——

CLARENCE. (*Enfolding* AUDREY.) Don't worry, Audrey. I'll pay for the dresses.

ERWIN. Oh, no you won't. I don't want you to pay for anything. (*Goes to sideboard; takes tobacco tin, takes out bills.*) Here, this is for your dresses. This ten was going to be for a split bamboo weak-fishing outfit. These three tens were going to be for a motor trip for the two of us and this ten was supposed to become a panama and a pair of sport shoes—but pay for the dresses. Don't forget to get a receipt. (*Picks up box, puts it back in cabinet.*)

AUDREY. Where are you going?

ERWIN. To the office—I'm late.

AUDREY. You've forgotten your necktie.

ERWIN. What's the difference? Who cares how I look? To hell with the tie.

AUDREY. Erwin!

ERWIN. And to hell with this house.

CLARENCE. What!

AUDREY. Erwin! You'll hurt Clarence's feelings.

ERWIN. And I won't apologize.

AUDREY. *Erwin.*

BLACK-OUT AND CURTAIN

ACT I

SCENE 2: *A barroom of the Lavillere Hotel. The bar is upstage, two thirds the distance. Telephone booth to* R. *Elevator door diagonally across from booth. Door to men's room off* R. *out of view, and door to hotel lobby* R. . . . *Door to street* L. *Stairs seen leading to street. This is really the basement of the Hotel.*
TIME: *About three in the afternoon.*

AT RISE: HARRY *the bartender is behind bar.* CHARLIE *and* FRANKIE *seated at table* D. R. *They have racing sheets spread out on table.* FRANKIE *is about half as tall as* CHARLIE. *He wears a derby and is smoking a large cigar.* CHARLIE *is smoking a cigarette. His gray hat is pushed off his forehead.*

HARRY. What'll you have, the same?
CHARLIE. Just make it one beer this time. (*Counts change.*) We'll split it, Frankie. (*To* HARRY.) We don't want to break a bill if we can help it—maybe we can figure out a horse to play on in this third race.
HARRY. That's all right by me.
FRANKIE. Geez, you'd think Patsy would call up or somethin'.
CHARLIE. It don't take all day to hock a belt buckle.
FRANKIE. Maybe it wasn't gold after all.
CHARLIE. He paid enough for it.
HARRY. (*Bringing beer to table.*) It just goes to show you how the luck will go. Lobster one day—beans the next. You three fellows were sittin' pretty—how much was it you ran up to last month?
CHARLIE. About four hundred bucks. Aw—we'll have it again.
FRANKIE. Sure.
HARRY. Geez, I could almost open my own place with that. I was tellin' the manager the other day—now the trouble with this place is—it looks too much like a speakeasy—if a thing is legal it should look legal—that's what I say—and another thing—when anybody takes a room at this hotel they don't come in here much—if they want to have a party—they take the bottle to the room. (*Phone.* HARRY *goes into booth.*)

(*Throughout following scene we see* HARRY *nod now and then through glass door of booth.*)

CHARLIE. (*Counting money.*) Two, three, four, five, six. Well, I know how I'm going to play my six bucks.
FRANKIE. Yeah?
CHARLIE. Yeah? I'm playing the surest thing I know . . . three bucks on Rose Cross to show.
FRANKIE. But Charlie, Rose Cross won't pay back anything much even if she wins . . . if you lay three bucks to place, you'd only get about ninety cents—so, if she shows, you're lucky to get two bits.
CHARLIE. Listen, we got to reserve our capital. Two bits is breakfast money anyways. How d'ya think we're going to eat? We can't get credit for a bet any more—let alone feed money. You know that!

FRANKIE. But you're puttin' up half your roll. Suppose Rose Cross don't come in?

CHARLIE. There's only five horses in the race. She ought to show at least.—This is a hell of a spot to be in. I wish Patsy would come back. Sometimes he gets some good ideas. Even Mabel ain't in her room. Did she go out with Patsy?

FRANKIE. No, she's doin' the same thing—she took out all her dresses and a parasol that's got a gold top. It's a good thing Patsy's got Mabel—he got forty-five bucks on that bracelet of hers yesterday.

CHARLIE. What do you mean it's a good thing Patsy's got Mabel? He bought all that stuff for her, didn't he?

FRANKIE. What I mean is—she's a good investment. (HARRY *comes out of booth and goes back to bar.* ERWIN *enters slowly down stairs.*) She's a nice kid, Mabel.

CHARLIE. Yeah, she's all right—well, the hell with all that. I got to bet.

HARRY. That was Gus on the phone. He wanted to find out if anybody wanted to bet the third race.

CHARLIE. Who copped that second?

HARRY. Fairweather.

CHARLIE. Fairweather, huh?

HARRY. Brass Monkey took the first. He paid eight to one. (*Looks at paper.*)

(ERWIN *takes* HARRY'S *pencil—makes two checks with it in his little book.* HARRY *looks at slip of paper.*)

CHARLIE. Musta been a sleeper.

HARRY. What'll it be?

ERWIN. (*Looking around.*) I don't think I'll meet anybody here ——

HARRY. What'll you have?

ERWIN. (*Going to bar.*) Scotch.

FRANKIE. I don't think I want to bet today.

CHARLIE. Now listen, we didn't play yesterday nor the day before—we got to bet today. We might as well break the ice.

ERWIN. (*To* HARRY.) I should be at the office.

HARRY. Takin' a couple hours for lunch, huh?

ERWIN. No. I mean I should have been at the office this morning.

HARRY. Oh.

CHARLIE. We could play it like this—say we put two dollars on Rose Cross to win—then we put—now let's see . . . (*He figures silently with a pencil.*)

HARRY. I guess you can always do what you like when you're in business for yourself.

ERWIN. Gosh, sometimes I wish I was in business for myself.

HARRY. I thought you was.

ERWIN. No, that's the trouble. I should have been at the office a long time ago. Let me have another drink.

HARRY. It's none of my business, brother, but don't you think you should go to the office while you're able to navigate?

ERWIN. (*Waves idea aside.*) I don't think I'll ever go to the office again. (*Rests chin on elbow at bar as his attention is drawn to table.*)

HARRY. Oh. (As if to say "It's as bad as that.")

CHARLIE. Maybe we should pass up the third. Does anything look good in the fourth?

HARRY. (*To* ERWIN.) They been sittin' there for an hour tryin' to decide on a horse to play.

ERWIN. Do you know them?

HARRY. Sure. They live in this hotel.

ERWIN. Do you think they'd mind if I gave them a horse?

HARRY. What's that again?

ERWIN. I said, do you think they would mind if I gave them a tip on the third race?

HARRY. Do you play the horses, too?

ERWIN. Me? No.

HARRY. Oh. Well, you see they're down to twelve bucks and I think it might be better if they made a choice themselves—because if they lost they wouldn't feel so good.

ERWIN. You mean they wouldn't like me?

HARRY. That's it.

FRANKIE. (ERWIN *turns.* FRANKIE *throws down racing paper.*) Aw, hell, do what you like, Charlie. I don't see anything good. I think I'll wait for Patsy. He might have somethin'.

CHARLIE. All right. I'm playin' Rose Cross.

ERWIN. (*Looks in book. Weaves to table.*) Excuse me, gentlemen, I see you're interested in horses. You should really play Semester in the third race.

CHARLIE. Yeah?

FRANKIE. Wheredja get that?

ERWIN. Oh, I have it right here.
FRANKIE. Semester ain't rated much with the boys.
HARRY. Hey! You better come back here and finish your drink.
CHARLIE. One of them long shot guys.
FRANKIE. Looks like a nut.
CHARLIE. Say, Harry, you better see if he can pay for his drinks. He might want to pay you with a tip.
ERWIN. You fellows have the wrong opinion of me. I was just trying to do you a favor. (*Pulls bill out of wallet.*) Look, twenty dollars. I can pay for more drinks than I ever drank in my whole life. (*To* HARRY.) Don't get me wrong. I don't drink much. But did you ever feel blue?
HARRY. Sure. Lots of times.
ERWIN. That's just the way I feel today. I got off the bus—and I just didn't care—I should be at the office—but my wife and brother-in-law —— You married?
HARRY. No.
ERWIN. Then you haven't got a brother-in-law. I got off the bus and I started for the office—and then I just didn't care any more.
CHARLIE. I'll put a dollar to win and one to show. Rose Cross.
FRANKIE. It's your six bucks, not mine.

(CHARLIE *starts for booth.*)

ERWIN. You should really play Semester in the third race.
CHARLIE. If it's all the same to you, pal, I'll play Rose Cross. (*Goes into booth.*)
ERWIN. (*Back to* HARRY.) That's the trouble. Nobody pays much attention to me. I think I'll have another drink. (ERWIN *pours drink.*) Say, Harry . . . your name is Harry, isn't it?
HARRY. Yes.
ERWIN. You are a very understanding sort of fellow—would *you* like to play Semester in the third race just to see what would happen?
HARRY. (*Laughs.*) I know what would happen.
ERWIN. Don't you bet on horses?
HARRY. Say, I wouldn't bet on a horse if I was ridin' him myself.
CHARLIE. Just got it down in time. (*Returns to table.*)
ERWIN. Harry, you're a gentleman. I'd like to see you make some money.
HARRY. So would I.

ERWIN. (*Takes out book.*) Now let's see what I have for the fourth race.

PATSY. (*Enters from street. He is a dapper young man in a blue suit, gray suede shoes and light hat. Has an air of authority.*) Hello, Harry.

HARRY. Hello, Patsy. The boys was worried about you.

PATSY. (*Sits.*) I been all over town. Interestin' how many guys never heard of you before when they know you lost your roll. Well, Frankie, what did you do?

FRANKIE. Nothin'.

CHARLIE. Frankie was waitin' to see of you knew somethin' good. I just played two bucks on Rose Cross.

PATSY. Two bucks?

CHARLIE. We only got twelve between us. Did you get much on your buckle?

PATSY. Couple bucks. Mabel come in yet?

CHARLIE. No—an' I called her room for you.

PATSY. Thanks. She's trying to raise something too.

ERWIN. (*Crossing to table and tapping* PATSY *on shoulder.*) I was telling them they should play Semester in the third race.

PATSY. (*To boys.*) Who's he?

CHARLIE. Just some drunk.

ERWIN. (*Starts back to bar, gets dizzy. More to himself.*) Semester in the third. Hasty Belle in the fourth. (*Suddenly feels sick.*)

HARRY. Hey—right back in there, brother.

ERWIN. Oh. (*Heads for lavatory. Exits.*)

(*Phone rings.* HARRY *shuts door after him and comes down behind bar.*)

CHARLIE. That's Gus. (*Goes into booth.*)

HARRY. Geez, the country's full of amateurs. That guy shouldn't drink much.

PATSY. He don't look like a drinker to me.

FRANKIE. He looks like a goof.

HARRY. No. He's a nice guy.

CHARLIE. (*Comes out of booth.*) Well, I'll be hit on the nose.

PATSY. What's the matter?

CHARLIE. Guess who won that race?—Semester.

PATSY. Well, what about it?

CHARLIE. Didn't you hear him? He's been trying to give us Semester for the last ten minutes.

FRANKIE. Say, how did that guy know?
HARRY. He kept looking in a little book ——
PATSY. What book?
HARRY. Here it is. This book.
PATSY. (*Crosses to bar.*) Let's see. (*Takes book.* CHARLIE, *then* FRANKIE *crosses to look.*) Geez—he's got them all figured out.
CHARLIE. What do you mean figured out?
PATSY. Here's yesterday's winners, and the day before—pages of races —— My God, he's got Brass Monkey for today—he come in —so did Fairweather and Semester.
FRANKIE. Aw, he maybe wrote them down after the races was run.
HARRY. Wrote them down nuts. I heard him tell you to bet Semester before you got the result.
CHARLIE. Yeah, that's right.
FRANKIE. (*Leans on bar.*) Maybe he's a handicapper.
PATSY. Now you know he don't look like a handicapper.
HARRY. He said somethin' about workin' in an office.
CHARLIE. What's he got for the fourth?
PATSY. Hasty Belle. He's got the fourth, fifth, sixth, seventh and eighth figured out.
FRANKIE. Hasty Belle, huh, maybe we ought to lay two bucks on him.
PATSY. Two bucks, nothin'. We'll play the works.

(FRANKIE *takes book.*)

CHARLIE. (*Going* L.) Wait a minute! Maybe it's a new kind of a racket.
PATSY. To hell with that. How much you got?
CHARLIE. I still got four bucks. I ain't been any place. (*Taking out money.*)
FRANKIE. (*Does same.*) I got six left.
PATSY. (*Crosses to* R. *of* CHARLIE.) And I got eight. (*Pulls out money.*) You put up your ten between you, that's eighteen bucks altogether. You take it around to Gus, Frankie, while this guy's in there. (*Turns to* FRANKIE *who joins him.*)
FRANKIE. But we don't know anything about him.
PATSY. Maybe he runs a service or somethin'. You go on around and I'll go in and talk to him.
HARRY. I'll bet he's sick as a pup.
PATSY. What the hell do I care?

FRANKIE. But suppose the horse loses?

PATSY. If he does Mabel will be in with some dough in time for the next race. It wouldn't be the first time we ever lost, would it? Now you go on around and I'll keep this guy busy in here. (*Turns* R.)

FRANKIE. (*Up steps.*) All right. What's the name of the horse again?

PATSY. Hasty Belle.

FRANKIE. (*On landing.*) I'll lay the eighteen bucks, but I ain't responsible if this goat don't come in. (*He goes.*)

HARRY. He kept tryin' to give *me* a horse.

PATSY. I'll see if he's still conscious. (*Exits.*)

HARRY. (CHARLIE *sits table up* L.) Say, it will be interestin' to know what the hell this is all about. He kept askin' me if I was married—now what would that have to do with horses? Hey, I don't want to forget to collect for those drinks.

MABEL. (*Enters from street. She is an ex-Follies girl, a bit faded and quite dumb.*) Hello, boys.

CHARLIE. H'ya, Mabel.

HARRY. Hello, Mabel.

MABEL. Patsy told me to meet him here. We had some business to talk over.

CHARLIE. That's all right, Mabel, we know where you been.

MABEL. (*Sits* R. *of table.*) Kinda embarrassing, isn't it, to always be hockin' things. Well, it's all over now. I haven't anything left to hock except the dress I got on. It wouldn't be worth much. . . . I couldn't hock it anyway because I haven't anything else left to wear . . . you know in case I had to go out some place.

CHARLIE. Oh, I think you can keep that, Mabel.

MABEL. Hasn't Patsy come in yet?

CHARLIE. Sure, he's come in. He's in there. (*Gestures with thumb.*)

MABEL. Oh! I'll wait for him then.

CHARLIE. He's pretty busy.

MABEL. Sure, I guess he is.

CHARLIE. I mean he's got somebody with him.

MABEL. Somebody with him—in the—in there?

CHARLIE. Yeah—some guy.

MABEL. What kind of a guy, Charlie?

CHARLIE. Oh, he's all right. He's a friend of Patsy's.

MABEL. Do I know him?

CHARLIE. I don't think so. You see—he knew Patsy in the old days

—you know—and he heard how the luck was—and . . . and—he just dropped in to tip Patsy off on some fixed races so Patsy could get straightened out. Isn't that right, Harry?
HARRY. Sounds all right, Charlie.
MABEL. You mean he fixes them?
CHARLIE. Yeah, that's it . . . he fixes them.
MABEL. But what are they doing in the Johnnie?
CHARLIE. Well, he got sick from the heat and some bum liquor . . . I mean he ain't used to drinkin'. Patsy used to be his best friend —— He's holding his head.

(MOSES *stops elevator and opens elevator door.* MOSES *is the colored elevator boy. He is quite heavy and wears a tight uniform.*)

FRANKIE. (*Enters.*) I put in that bet. Hello, Mabel.
MABEL. Hello ——
FRANKIE. Where are they?
MABEL. They're in the Johnnie.
MOSES. (*Stepping out of elevator.*) One pint rye, bottle ginger ale. (*Looks at table.*) Good afternoon.
FRANKIE. Hello, Moses ——
MOSES. How is the horses?
CHARLIE. O. K. How are the numbers?
MOSES. Fine and dandy. I is playin' a combination I seen on a two dollar bill today. I just see it. (*Speaks as he crosses to bar.*)
HARRY. (Gives him order.) Somebody havin' a party?
MOSES. The couple in 312 just wakin' up —— (*Crossing back with tray.*) Mr. Charlie, I was on the third floor and the maid asked me if it was all right to make up your room and I said yeah —— (*Goes back into elevator.*)
CHARLIE. Thanks, Moses.

(*Moses shuts elevator door.*)

PATSY. (*Enters.*) He's pretty sick. Did you lay the bets, Frankie?
FRANKIE. On the nose.
PATSY. That's right. Well, Mabel, how did you make out?
MABEL. (*Rising and going to* PATSY.) I went down to this place on Eighth Avenue like you told me and I unwrapped the dresses . . .
PATSY. Yeah?
MABEL. . . . which were very good as you recall . . . and he said they wasn't so good and I told him they was and then he said they

was out of style and I showed him the price tags with the date on which was only last week and he said, "How much do you want?" and I said, "How much do you think they're worth?" and he said that isn't the question, he said he might be able to sell them for forty dollars but that they was only worth eight dollars to him and I said that wasn't the right attitude to take and he said, "The hell with the attitude, will you take the eight bucks?"

PATSY. Did you take it?

MABEL. Yes.

PATSY. Good.

MABEL. (*Gives him money.*) Then I asked somebody on the street where I could sell a parasol with a gold head and they said I would have to go to the assay office and I said I wouldn't do that. (*Crosses; pushes elevator bell.*)

CHARLIE. Ertznay . . . you can sell that any place.

FRANKIE. Gold? Certainly you can sell that any place. That's the basic metal, ain't it?

PATSY. Frankie, take this eight bucks and put it on More Anon in the fifth.

CHARLIE. More Anon?

FRANKIE. But we don't know the results of the fourth yet or anything. How do we know ——

PATSY. I know a lot now. I been talkin' to him.

FRANKIE. All right then, if you're sure. (*Starts to go.*) The fourth is on pretty soon.

PATSY. We'll call up.

(FRANKIE *goes out street door. Elevator door opens.*)

MOSES. Goin' up?

MABEL. Yeah, my feet are tired. I'm goin' up to change my shoes,

PATSY. Gee, honey, I think it's swell about this friend of yours fixin' the races for us so we can get a roll again.

PATSY. (*At bar.*) Yeah . . . yeah . . . Sweetheart, ain't that somethin'? We'll see you later then.

MABEL. All right. (*Goes. Elevator rises.*)

PATSY. What didja tell her, Charlie, so I'll know?

CHARLIE. I told her he was a friend of yours who was fixin' some races for you because he heard how you was broke . . . you two is old buddies . . . he used to be your best friend.

PATSY. (ERWIN *enters.* PATSY *goes to him.*) How do you feel now, Erwin? (*Turns to boys.*) His name is Erwin.

HARRY. I knew it would be somethin' like that.

ERWIN. (PATSY *leads him to chair.*) I think I feel a little bit better now.

PATSY. (CHARLIE *rises.*) Sit down in this nice chair.

CHARLIE. I hope he don't have to leave soon.

PATSY. He's not leavin'. He's stayin' here till he gets straightened out.

ERWIN. I forgot to pay for the drinks.

HARRY. (*Coming around to him.*) Aw, that's all right.

ERWIN. How much is it?

HARRY. One dollar, even.

ERWIN. Can you break a twenty?

HARRY. Sure. (*Takes bill to register.*)

FRANKIE. (*Enters. Crosses* R. *to phone booth; speaks while he dials.*) The bets are in. I'm calling Gus. It's post time for the fourth. (*Dials phone leaving booth door open.*)

PATSY. We had a long talk. His name is Erwin somebody. He picks those horses for fun. He says it's a hobby.

CHARLIE. Hobby, huh?

FRANKIE. Hello, Gus . . . this is Frankie. Hasty Belle is 4-1. . . . Yeah, Gus.

HARRY. (*Brings change to* ERWIN.) Gee, I hope he's not a nut; you know how a guy can get about horses.

FRANKIE. Yeah, Gus, I'm here . . . They're at the quarter ——

HARRY. Here's your change.

ERWIN. Thanks.

(HARRY *goes back to bar.*)

FRANKIE. Yeah, yeah, Joybird . . . Little Lie . . . Post Script . . . I got it . . . Hasty Belle in that order . . .

PATSY. This is the fourth.

CHARLIE. The one Hasty Belle is in.

PATSY. He ain't done much this season.

CHARLIE. Yeah, I know.

FRANKIE. Joybird up at the half. . . . Who comes up? . . . Little Lie. . . . Now Post Script . . . neck and neck . . . yes . . . still that way? . . . They're in the stretch . . . yes, yes. . . . He's past . . . he's past . . .

ERWIN. (*Opens eyes.*) What's the matter?

PATSY. (*Crosses to booth.*) Horse race.

who's past? . . . Joybird? Hasty Belle . . . passes Joybird . . . she does? . . . O. K. (*Hangs up, turns to others.*) Hasty Belle wins.

CHARLIE. Hasty Belle wins.
PATSY. Huh?

ERWIN. What's the matter?
CHARLIE. Hasty Belle wins.
ERWIN. What do you know about that?
CHARLIE. (*Looks at sheet.*) He ran out of the money the last five starts.
PATSY. (*Bangs on bar.*) Boy!

(*Suddenly* FRANKIE, CHARLIE *and* PATSY *look at* ERWIN.)

ERWIN. (*Embarrassed.*) Well, he won. (*Searches pocket.*) Where is my little book?
FRANKIE. (*Across table.*) Here I was holdin' it for you.
ERWIN. Just make a check beside Hasty Belle.
HARRY. Here, I'll buy you a drink. (*Puts glass on bar.*)
ERWIN. I'm not sure I can drink any more.
PATSY. Sure you can. Frankie, collect and put it all on "Rip Van Winkle."
FRANKIE. I'll put up the same amount for the three of us. (*Exits.*)
PATSY. (*Strolling upstage, then back.*) That's the idea—that bracelet don't suit Mabel so hot anyways. I think I'll get her a platinum wrist watch. Don't you want to bet Erwin?
ERWIN. I never bet.
PATSY. You don't?
ERWIN. No. I just spent forty-eight dollars.
HARRY. Not in here.
ERWIN. No, before I left home. Forty-eight dollars. Now I'm not going fishing.
CHARLIE. Aw.
ERWIN. Forty-eight dollars and he's going to buy a platinum rich wast. Women. It's all the same, isn't it, no matter how you look at it?
HARRY. Sure, it's all the same.
ERWIN. (*Rises.*) Well, I think I'll go.
PATSY. Where you goin'?
ERWIN. Oh, I have to be at the office.

CHARLIE. (*Rises.*) You can't go to any office like that. (*Turning* ERWIN.)

HARRY. You'll lose your job.

PATSY. Sure. You work, huh? Everybody's goin' to go home pretty soon.

ERWIN. Huh?

PATSY. People who work in offices will be goin' home pretty soon.

ERWIN. Mr. Carver would still be there. He'll be waiting for me.

PATSY. (*Seats* ERWIN, CHARLIE *stands.*) Sit down a second. I want to talk to you.—How much do you make a week?

ERWIN. Well, I get regular $40 and then there's extra. At fifty cents a line sometimes I sell stuff and that brings it up to forty-six or fifty some weeks not counting the postage stamps and the envelopes and maybe this week it might come to forty-nine.

CHARLIE. (*Sits.*) Don't you want to wait and see how these races come out?

ERWIN. Oh, no. I can look at the results on my way home.

PATSY. (*Sits.*) So you make about fifty bucks a week. That's eight fifty a day. Now why don't you stay here and I'll give you ten per cent on everything I play and Charlie and Frankie will too.

CHARLIE. Sure.

ERWIN. That sounds all right as far as the money is concerned ——

PATSY. What's the matter? We bet on horses, that's our business, but you like to pick them—so we pay you for it—if we bet, say, twenty dollars on a horse and he pays back say, eight to one . . . we get one hundred and sixty dollars—you get sixteen dollars . . . ten per cent. . . . That's about twice as much as you'd make if you worked all day.

CHARLIE. You see—we take a chance too. Suppose the horse loses?

ERWIN. (*Rises.*) Yes . . . but I don't think I want to stay here.

PATSY. Why not? . . . You can't go to the office like that. We'll call up. (*Placing* ERWIN *back in chair.*)

CHARLIE. What's the number, Erwin? I'll call him ——

ERWIN. B. O. 4–6752.

PATSY. I'll call your boss and tell him you won't be in.

HARRY. I guess he knows that by now.

CHARLIE. We'll tell him anyway. (*Dials number.*)

PATSY. We'll tell him you don't feel good.

CHARLIE. (*As he stops dialing and puts receiver to ear.*) Who shall I ask for?

ERWIN. Mr. J. G. Carver.

CHARLIE. (*Into phone.*) Mr. Carver please. Oh, you're Mr. Carver —well, Mr. Carver —— (*To* ERWIN.) What's your last name, Erwin?

ERWIN. Trowbridge.

CHARLIE. (*Into phone.*) Erwin Trowbridge won't be in today . . . (ERWIN *rises*—PATSY *seats him.*) he got sick on his way to the office . . . yeah . . . terrible . . . he's in the drug store now . . . been here for a long time . . . we been workin' over him. . . . Me! I'm the Pharmastist . . . yeah . . . What? . . . I'll tell him. Good-bye. (*Hangs up; comes down, sits* L. *of* ERWIN.) He says that's O. K. because there wouldn't be no use comin' in this late anyways. He says as long as you can get your work done by tomorrow that's jake by him. If you don't feel so hot tomorrow you better send them anyways. Does that make sense to you?

ERWIN. Yes. I should get those verses written.

PATSY. You a song writer?

ERWIN. No. Greeting verse. I'm late for Mother's Day.

PATSY. You're what?

ERWIN. (*Looking at* PATSY.) I have to catch up on Mother's Day.

PATSY. We understand, Erwin. You got an aspirin, Harry? (*Going to bar.*)

HARRY. (*Passes aspirin and glass of water over bar.*) Sure.

PATSY. Now you just sit there and relax.

HARRY. On the house.

CHARLIE. I'll give it to him. (*Taking them.*)

FRANKIE. (*Runs in.*) Hey, listen. What do you think—I played the fifth . . . one two three . . . like in the book.

PATSY. Yeah . . . yeah . . . so what?

FRANKIE. They come in.

PATSY. One two three?

FRANKIE. One two three.

CHARLIE. Can you top that?

PATSY. You hear that, Erwin? Go on take it down. What's a headache to you, eh, Erwin? You're makin' money. (*Shaking* ERWIN *by knees.*)

ERWIN. (*When he recovers.*) Have I made eight fifty yet?

PATSY. Eight fifty! About eighty-eight fifty. (CHARLIE *crosses to bar with glass and sips as he crosses.*) How much you bet altogether, Frankie?

FRANKIE. (*Looking in book.* PATSY *with* FRANKIE.) Let's see—I got back on the fifth at ten each—84 and 41 and 15 that's $140 each, plus what we got on "Hasty Belle" that we played on "More Anon"—altogether that brings a total of $245 each.

CHARLIE. There ain't that much money. (*Crossing to bar.*) Harry, could you make up a turkey sandwich?

HARRY. (*At bar.*) I haven't sold a turkey sandwich in a week. How about cheese?

PATSY. We ain't got time to fool around with food.

FRANKIE. We ought to play all the races—1-2-3.

PATSY. Erwin's only got the fifth figured that way. Let's see the sheets, Frankie.

(*They start looking at handicap sheets.*)

ERWIN. (*Who has been sitting, head in hands.*) Could I have a pencil?

PATSY. Sure, sure, Erwin, here's a pencil.

CHARLIE. (*Taking envelope out of pocket.*) Here's some paper——

ERWIN. (*Searching through clothes.*) Thanks, I have some paper.

(ERWIN *goes to work writing rapidly.*)

PATSY. Got a flash, hey, Erwin?

CHARLIE. (*Holding up hand and speaking in almost a whisper.*) We better not talk much.

(*The three quietly back upstage.*)

FRANKIE. (*Whispering.*) I been looking through the book and I see Erwin has a record of parlays but he ain't got none for today.

CHARLIE. (*Holds up hand.*) Look, he got somethin' hot.

PATSY. What you got, Erwin?

ERWIN. (*More to himself.*) I got one.

FRANKIE. Let's have it.

ERWIN. What?

PATSY. (*Coming down quietly.*) Let's hear what you got.

ERWIN. Oh, no. You wouldn't be interested in this.

CHARLIE. Sure we would. Let's hear it.

ERWIN. (PATSY *and* CHARLIE *sink down into chairs on each side.*) Well, I think it will do. Here it is.

"At Christmas Tide your hair was gray
But memories chased your cares away,
Now lovingly in my simple way
I send you love on Mother's Day."

Mother's Day No. 16.

PATSY. (*Giving* ERWIN *a long look.*) Yeah . . . yeah . . . that's all right, Erwin. That's elegant—what is that, Erwin?

ERWIN. That's a Mother's Day verse.

PATSY. You mean you just thought that up?

ERWIN. Yes.

PATSY. Since you been sittin' there?

ERWIN. Sure.

PATSY. Geez, can you imagine that, Frankie?

FRANKIE. (*Turns to* HARRY.) Weird, ain't it?

CHARLIE. (*Stands; snaps fingers.*) Why don't you ask him about the horses?

PATSY. Yeah. We thought you was figurin' some parlay. You know, like you have in your book.

ERWIN. No, sir. I have work to do. (*Rises.*) I have fifty more of those to do. How did that one sound? All right?

CHARLIE. (*Pats him.*) That was the nuts. I wish you'd dope out some parlays . . . you know . . . just for fun.

PATSY. (*Knocks* CHARLIE'S *arm down.*) Leave him alone—leave him alone—let him do whatever he wants. (*Seating him in chair.*) You go ahead, Erwin, write some more of them Mother's Day gags. . . . Where's the roll, Frankie? (*Sits.*)

FRANKIE. Here. (*Puts bills on table.*)

CHARLIE. (*Muses.*) You know I like that. (*Sits.*) "At Christmas Tide your hair was gray."

PATSY. Suppose you run down and wait around and get paid off on the sixth.

FRANKIE. O. K., Patsy. I don't mind at all. (*He goes off street door.*)

(MABEL *enters from elevator.*)

PATSY. Mabel, guess what I got for you. Look. (*Gives her money.*) You can go next door and get your bracelet out of hock.

MABEL. No foolin'. Are you sure if I get it out I won't have to put it back in the morning? I only hocked it yesterday and I'd feel so funny if I put it back in tomorrow.

PATSY. Sugar, you won't ever have to hock that bracelet again. Oh, Mabel, this is Erwin. Erwin is here to give us a helping hand.

MABEL. Pleased to meet you.

ERWIN. How do you do?

MABEL. (*Sits on* PATSY'S *knees.*) Charlie was telling me about you, how you're going to fix the races just for us. I think it's just wonderful.

HARRY. Hey, Patsy, how about settin' 'em up? I'm supposed to work here.

PATSY. Sure, Harry, rye for me, same for Erwin.

CHARLIE. Same here.

MABEL. Rye with plenty of ginger ale—I haven't been eatin' regular lately—I don't want to get tight.

PATSY. You're going to eat tonight, Mabel.

MABEL. Gee, I'm glad you looked us up.

ERWIN. "When I was young and on your knee ——"

MABEL. What?

CHARLIE. Sh—sh.

PATSY. Did you say somethin', Erwin?

ERWIN. How does that sound?

"When I was young and on your knee
You told a nursery rhyme to me.
But now I've grown a man to be
I send my love in rhyme to thee."

Mother's Day No. 17. (*Writes it down.*)

MABEL. What is that?

PATSY. (*Taking* MABEL *by the arm to bar.*) It's kind of hard to explain. (*Embarrassed to think he is associating with a sentimental verse writer.*) That's a sort of a code.

HARRY. There yuh are.

MABEL. Huh!

PATSY. A message.

MABEL. Gee, Patsy, this is swell—it's like—it's like spies talk in that magazine story I was readin'—(HARRY *brings tray of drinks to table.*) now what was the name of that ——

HARRY. Here we are. (*Serves drinks.*)

PATSY. (*Takes two drinks off tray* HARRY *holds.*) Mabel, how would you like to see a musical tonight?

MABEL. (*Taking one of the drinks from* PATSY.) I don't know. Let's go somewhere else. There's none of the old crowd in it at all any more.

PATSY. Bet you could get back if you wanted to.

MABEL. Do you really think so, Patsy?

PATSY. (*Placing empty glasses on bar during speech.*) Sure —— (*Pats her hip.*) Take off a few pounds—you know—here and there. It would be a cinch. Here you are, Harry. (*Gives him bill.*) But I got other plans for you, Mabel. You don't want to be tied down. How do we know where we'll be—New Orleans, Lexington, Chicago——

(HARRY *rings cash register.*)

MABEL. How do you mean, Patsy?
PATSY. That depends on what agreement me and Erwin can come to. (*Walks to foot of stairs with* MABEL.) Now you run upstairs and get your bracelet out and we'll celebrate tonight. Just you and me. How would that be? We'll get dressed and have dinner at Lindy's and make a night of it.
MABEL. Get dressed—all right—but this is the only dress I got.
PATSY. Get another one. (*Pats her behind. Gives her money.*) Happy days are here again, huh, Mabel. (MABEL *goes up stairs.* PATSY *returns to bar.*) She's as happy as a kid. Buy Erwin another drink, Harry—on me.
CHARLIE. (*Watching* ERWIN *write.*) How many of them things do you have to write?
ERWIN. Fifty more.
CHARLIE. This week?
ERWIN. By tomorrow.
PATSY. Do you think you can do it?
ERWIN. I have to—my job.
PATSY. Job—huh—say, I bet you'll retire on these ten per cents. (*Crosses and pushes elevator bell.*)
FRANKIE. (*Runs in.*) I got the sixth.
CHARLIE. The sixth. (*Ad lib.*)
FRANKIE. He comes in——(*Tosses bills on table. Has bills in both coat pockets.*)
PATSY. It ain't true. Look at that, Erwin. Your brains did that. Don't that make you excited? (*Sits* L.)
ERWIN. There's a lot of money there, I guess. I can see some twenty dollar bills.
FRANKIE. Twenties, huh? I bet ten each like I said. My Blaze paid back six sixty for two so that was thirty-three dollars each and Rip Van Winkle paid seven forty for two. That comes to——

(HARRY *sets drink before* ERWIN.)

PATSY. Five times seven forty.
CHARLIE. (*Excited.*) Thirty-seven . . .
FRANKIE. Altogether it comes to seventy dollars each.

PATSY. Now you get seven dollars from me plus what you got before and you get the same from Frankie and Charlie too. That's as much as you'd make in a week writing them Mother's Day Number Fifteens.

(*Elevator stops.*)

MOSES. Goin' up?

PATSY. You count out the dough, Charlie. I'll be right back. I'm going to celebrate and pay my bill. (*Exit elevator.*)

CHARLIE. That's ten for Frank—ten for Patsy—ten for me. (*Continues this silently as* MABEL *comes in from street.*)

MABEL. (*Enters, sits* R.) I got my bracelet out. (*Holding up arm.*) Hello! Where's Patsy?

CHARLIE. He'll be right back. He went to pay the hotel bill.

MABEL. What bank was all this in?

CHARLIE. Horses.

MABEL. (*Sits and looks at* ERWIN *with genuine admiration. He sips drink.*) You mean you won all this since I left, Erwin?

CHARLIE. This is just from the sixth race.

MABEL. Gee, that must take a lot of nerve—to fix races.

ERWIN. Oh, I don't know.

MABEL. How long did it take you?

ERWIN. About an hour.

MABEL. How did you get in this racket, Erwin? On account of conditions? I'll bet you were making out all right before. I'd never think you were in rackets if I didn't see you here with Patsy and the boys and that roll there. I'll bet you never have to worry about making a living.

FRANKIE. How about a drink for everybody?

MABEL. Sure.

CHARLIE. O. K.

ERWIN. I don't think I could drink anymore.

FRANKIE. I'm buying them. We ought to celebrate.

ERWIN. But I don't feel so good.

MABEL. It wouldn't be any fun if you don't drink too—on account of we'll really be drinking to you—you know what I mean—fixing the races and all that.

ERWIN. All right then.

(*Elevator opens.*)

FRANKIE. Four drinks.

PATSY. (*Enters from elevator.*) Make it five. (*Points to bills.*) How's that look to you, Mabel? This mine, Charlie? (*Picking pile off table.*)
CHARLIE. That's yours.
PATSY. That's fine. Mabel, let's see your bracelet. You and me is going to be back in circulation tonight. How's about it?
HARRY. (*Serves drinks.*) Here we are.
MABEL. It feels like old times again, huh, Patsy? I was just saying we ought to drink this to Erwin because he's helping us out like this. Come on, Erwin . . . bottoms up.

(*They all drink.*)

ERWIN. Oh, sure. (*He drinks.*)
PATSY. Sugar, suppose you go along and start to get dolled up, and knock on my door when you're ready.
MABEL. All right, Patsy. Well, good-bye . . . (*Going to elevator.* ERWIN *rises.*) Oh, Patsy, I saw a dress in a window I want to show you later on.
PATSY. Anything you say goes, Mabel . . . dress, coat, hat . . . I might even name a horse after you.
MABEL. Good-bye, Erwin.

(*Elevator door closes.*)

PATSY. Say, do you guys realize how lucky we are? Twenty-four hours ago we owed ourselves money . . . now look at us . . . we got the makings of a million dollar bank roll. But we got to keep our mouths shut and Erwin has to play along with us. You hear that, Erwin? (*Drops arm.*) Geez, he's passed out.
HARRY. What did you think he was, a sponge?
PATSY. Listen, Harry. He's staying here with us tonight. Then he can pick the entries for tomorrow's races, get it?
HARRY. Sure, I get it.
CHARLIE. (*Rises and fans* ERWIN.) Hey, you don't think we'll get in any trouble, do you?
PATSY. Trouble? We're doing him a favor. My God, he's been working for fifty cents a line and here he's already made as much as he would in a week. Ring for the elevator, Charlie.
FRANKIE. But suppose something . . . (ERWIN *almost falls out of chair. They catch him.*) Is he all right?

(HARRY *looks at his eyes.*)

PATSY. He's all right. He just passed out, hey, Harry?
HARRY. Yeah. Yeah. He'll be O. K. He'll be all right.
PATSY. Say, you're not going to say anything about this, are you, Harry?
HARRY. Hell no. I just want you to play this five bucks for me on the last race. This is the first time I ever came face to face with a sure thing.
FRANKIE. But suppose somebody finds out about it?
PATSY. (*Placing* ERWIN'S *head in his arms at table.*) Say, what's the matter with you guys? You got a yellow streak all of a sudden? He should be tickled to death. We're giving him a break. Suppose Leo's crowd had ever discovered him? He'd never see his wife again. They'd take him from track to track like a horse.
CHARLIE. I guess that's right.
PATSY. All we want to do is run up a bank roll, then to hell with the bookies . . . I'm going to get myself a stable and do this thing right.
MOSES. Goin' up.
PATSY. Here, give us a hand, will you, boys? (*Ad libs.*) Moses, he's a friend of ours just passed out. He's staying in my room tonight.

(*Ad libs.*)

(*As they put* ERWIN *in elevator.*)

CURTAIN

Orchestra plays "Happy Days Are Here Again"

ACT II

SCENE 1: *Ozone Heights.*

TIME: *The next morning.*

ORCHESTRA *plays "Some One of These Days" before curtain goes up and as it rises.*

AT RISE: AUDREY *sits alone, trying not to cry. She wipes her eyes, bites her lip, hits pillow of divan with her fist. Phone rings. She leaps to her feet and rushes to it.*

AUDREY. (*In phone.*) Hello. (*Disappointedly.*) Oh, yes, good morning, Mrs. Marple. We'd be delighted—at least I think we would—well, I can't ask him just now—he isn't here.—Well, he didn't come home last night—oh, no—nothing wrong—(*Sniffs.*) only he just didn't come home—business of course. . . . He and Mr. Carver . . . that's his boss—they have so many things to talk over, I suppose . . . and I'll ask him if he comes home today.—Oh, yes, of course he'll be here—I just slipped. Thank you, Mrs. Marple. (*Hangs up.*) Oh, Erwin—where are you?

(CLARENCE *enters aggressively.*)

CLARENCE. Showed up yet? (*She shakes her head.*) Didn't even phone. (*Shakes her head.*) Didn't hear from him at all, huh?

AUDREY. (*Between sobs.*) Mrs. Marple phoned . . .

CLARENCE. Yes?

AUDREY. Invited us to a party, but he may not even be here. (*Sobs.*)

CLARENCE. Well, if he isn't, I'll go with you.

AUDREY. Oh, dear. (*Sobs worse.*)

CLARENCE. (*Walks back and forth.*) He's the last fellow in the world I'd expect to do such a thing.

AUDREY. Do what thing?

CLARENCE. But in a way, I always knew he was that kind.

AUDREY. What are you talking about?

CLARENCE. Did you phone him at the office?

AUDREY. Erwin doesn't like me to phone his office.

CLARENCE. That's just a gag. What's his number? Huh, I can see through that. (*At desk.*) This it?

AUDREY. He won't like it.

CLARENCE. (*Grimly.*) This is just one of the things he isn't going to like. (*In phone.*) Bogardus 4-6752. I've got quite a few surprising revelations for you.

AUDREY. I don't want any revelations. I just want Erwin.

CLARENCE. (*Sits. In phone.*) I'd like to speak to Mr. Trowbridge—please—Erwin Trowbridge. . . . No? Is that so? . . . Oh, he didn't. I thank you very much——

AUDREY. What did they say?

CLARENCE. Mr. Carver isn't there.

AUDREY. Oh, Clarence—I don't care anything about Mr. Carver.

CLARENCE. Neither is Erwin. What's more he didn't come to work at all yesterday.

AUDREY. It's all my fault.

CLARENCE. What do you mean it's all your fault?

AUDREY. I shouldn't have bought those dresses. I knew he wouldn't like it.

CLARENCE. Oh, what right has a worm like that to object anyhow?

AUDREY. (*With tearful dignity.*) Erwin is not a worm—I don't like you to say such things about him.

CLARENCE. I told you not to marry him. Didn't I? Remember what I said to you? I said—"Don't marry him." You were stubborn. All right. I won't say anything about it. It's all past now. You could have married Charley Blanchard, don't forget that. There's a man for you—I spotted him as a comer at the first Kiwanis luncheon and where is he now? Seventy-five dollars a week and one per cent of all sales on his hardware accessories in upper New York and northern New Jersey. And where is Erwin?

AUDREY. (*Sobbing.*) I don't know—I wish I did.—Oh, Erwin!

(*Sinks on settee* R. C.)

CLARENCE. I'll tell you then—he's left you.

AUDREY. He has not.

CLARENCE. I had a feeling there was something funny about him when he went out of here. He wouldn't look me in the eye.

AUDREY. That wasn't it at all.

CLARENCE. He kept turning away from me.

AUDREY. He doesn't like to look at you—he told me so.

CLARENCE. I might have known he'd treat us like that. I help him along—I let him have a house on easy payment plan—do everything I can for him—does he come to me with a good thing? No—just quietly makes his little cleaning and then leaves us all flat.

AUDREY. What are you talking about?
CLARENCE. Brass Monkey won yesterday.
AUDREY. Who's Brass Monkey?
CLARENCE. The horse——He had a sure tip. That little book of his was full of sure tips. He's been cleaning up. All the time he's been playing poor and talking about how he couldn't afford things, he's been rich—he's had winnings enough in the last few weeks to spend the rest of his life loafing.—He's got deposits in a dozen savings banks—when I saw that little book yesterday it all came across me clear—in fact I went down to the bookies in the afternoon to put a thousand dollars on Brass Monkey and then I was afraid of some trickery and I changed my mind. God damn it. (*Crosses to* C.)
AUDREY. Why Clarence, I never heard you swear before.
CLARENCE. But the worm had his roll on that race—he had every cent—and he cleaned up and you'll never see him again.
AUDREY. You don't understand him—you don't understand him at all.
CLARENCE. (*Comes back to her.*) Why couldn't he have come to me as man to man and told me about it? That would have been the thing to do.—No, but he's selfish—keeps it all to himself—wouldn't look me in the eye—I knew something was wrong.—Eight to one it paid—but that worm held out on me.
AUDREY. He's not a worm. (*Violent.*) You shut up. You treat him awful, and I don't blame him for getting mad—and he never liked living in your old house anyhow. (*Phone.* AUDREY *answers it. Sits on chair* L. *of telepone table.*) Yes?—Oh, oh, Mr. Carver—yes, this is Mrs. Trowbridge.—No, I—haven't. I don't know.
CLARENCE. Do you want me to talk to him?
AUDREY. He had the verses with him—a drug store? . . .
CLARENCE. What did he say?
AUDREY. Yes, of course I will. (*Hangs up.*) Mr. Carver is awful mad (*Rises.*) because the verses aren't there yet. He says Erwin telephoned him yesterday from a drug store and said he didn't feel well. (*Looks up suddenly.*) He's lying in some hospital—sick—or in the back of some drug store. (*Rushes and picks up phone.*)
CLARENCE. What are you going to do?
AUDREY. (*In phone.*) Give me the Ozone Heights Police Department.
CLARENCE. (*Trying to stop her by placing hand on shoulder.*) Audrey!

AUDREY. (*Throwing off his hand.*) Leave me alone. This is Mrs. Erwin Trowbridge, No. 1 Dobbins Drive . . . I wish to report a missing person . . . yes, my husband . . . he didn't come home last night.

BLACK-OUT

Orchestra plays "All Alone"

ACT II

SCENE 2: *The hotel room.*

TIME: *Noon next day.*

Room in the Lavillere Hotel. Door to elevator and hall upstage to L. *Door to bathroom* U. R. *Bed upstage* R. *Window above head of bed. Night table next to bed. Chifforobe* D. R. *Closet* D. L., *phone on table* D. S. L. *Chairs, etc., sheets of writing paper on floor.*

AT RISE: ERWIN *discovered in bed. He sits up and groans. He has on union suit.* CHARLIE *enters from bathroom with wet towel.*

CHARLIE. How are you?

ERWIN. Where did everybody go?

CHARLIE. (*Places towel on* ERWIN'S *forehead.*) Don't worry—they'll be back. How's that feel?

ERWIN. Pretty good—but I don't feel so good.

FRANKIE. (*Enters from door with tomato juice.* PATSY *follows him a second later.*) Here, drink this.

PATSY. Drink it. (ERWIN *is bewildered.*) Drink all you can.

ERWIN. I don't think I can drink anything. (*Sighs.*) Oh, my head. What are all those papers on the floor?

CHARLIE. (*Picking them up.*) Those jingles of yours. Don't you remember? You wrote half the night.

FRANKIE. (*Picking too.*) Three—four—five.

ERWIN. How many did I do?

CHARLIE. I got twenty-two here.

FRANKIE. Six—seven—eight.

PATSY. There's about ten more in the bathroom.

ERWIN. I must have written nearly the whole sixty-seven.

CHARLIE. You certainly did.

ERWIN. I don't remember anything about it.

CHARLIE. You kept me awake the whole night.

PATSY. Feel better now?

ERWIN. (*Nods.*) Say, I must have gotten drunk. (*Looking around.*) Where am I?

PATSY. You're in the Lavillere Hotel. You passed out on us last night. We had to bring you up here.

ERWIN. What time is it?

CHARLIE. It's after twelve o'clock.

ERWIN. What! Thought you said it was daybreak. . . . I must go to the office. (*Starts to get out of bed.*)

(PATSY *pushes him back, giving* CHARLIE *a dirty look.*)

CHARLIE. You can't get up now.

FRANKIE. Easy now pal.

PATSY. You can't go to the office like that. You look like the devil. You'll lose your job.

ERWIN. But Mr. Carver must have these verses today.

PATSY. He'll have 'em today. One of us will take 'em around. There's nothin' to worry about—(*Winks at boys.*) I just had him on the phone. He said if you don't feel good—you can stay in bed all day.

ERWIN. I guess I was in a bad way—you see I never drink. Where are my clothes?

CHARLIE. In the bathroom.

ERWIN. (*Looks at bathroom.*) I must go in there a minute. I feel better now that I know the verses are practically done. Do they look all right? (*Sits up.*)

CHARLIE. They're swell. I wish I could say things like that in poetry . . . especially if you're with a gal. It makes it romantic like—sort of breaks the ice.

ERWIN. Oh yes.

CHARLIE. You know, you don't want to start right off and say, "How about it, Baby?"

ERWIN. You better get a big envelope and put all the verses in and take them personal to Mr. Carver—he's waiting for them.

PATSY. You take them, Frankie.

FRANKIE. Where is the joint?

ERWIN. The Holly Cheer Greeting Co., Inc., in the Wedgewood Building. You walk down Sixth Avenue ——

FRANKIE. I know where it is. I used to know a tomato on the tenth floor.

ERWIN. Our office is 909.

PATSY. O. K. Now get dressed and wash up and you'll feel like a new man.

ERWIN. Frankie, be sure Mr. Carver gets the verses himself.

PATSY. Don't worry about it.

ERWIN. Oh, but it's very important.

PATSY. Listen, you're going to make more money dopin' horses than you ever made. Now go on and get under a cold shower so you'll be in shape to pick the horses today.

(ERWIN *gets out of bed; crosses to bathroom door.*)

ERWIN. (*Turns to* PATSY.) Horses! Oh, I don't think I'll have time. I have to call my wife and I must see Mr. Carver later on ——

CHARLIE. You can do all that afterwards.

PATSY. Go on, get straightened up. Meantime I'll count out that money I owe you.

ERWIN. Money?

PATSY. A hundred and twelve dollars—I think it is. Yeah, that's right.

ERWIN. You owe me?

PATSY. Certainly. Don't you recall the agreement? We said we'd give you ten per cent of all we won.

ERWIN. I remember something like that . . . (*Sits on corner of bed.*) but I thought you said eight dollars and fifty cents . . . you mean to say I made one hundred and twelve dollars just picking the horses!

CHARLIE. That's right.

ERWIN. Well—gee—I—you mean if I picked them again today I might make that much again ——?

FRANKIE. Maybe more. (*Sits end bed next* ERWIN.)

ERWIN. But even that much again. That would be two hundred and twenty-four dollars . . . why with that I could tell Clarence to go to hell.

CHARLIE. Who's Clarence?

ERWIN. My brother-in-law.

FRANKIE. You could tell a lot of people.

ERWIN. It's just Clarence that I've been thinking about.

PATSY. Then you mean you'll pick them?

ERWIN. Yes, (*Rises.*) I—I'd like to very much. I'll just go in and get dressed. (*Goes into bathroom.*)

PATSY. We're set.

FRANKIE. Sure. (*Sits.*)

CHARLIE. (*Walks to desk.*) I don't know. I wouldn't be too certain. I'm worried.

PATSY. You're always crabbing. If it's rainin' you're afraid of wet feet; if it's shinin', the sun gets in your eyes.

FRANKIE. What you worried about now? Everything is going fine, ain't it?

CHARLIE. That's the trouble. Everything is going too good. I'm worried. How do we know? (*Turns.*) For instance, how long it takes him to dope 'em out? Maybe he has to work on 'em for a couple of weeks ahead of time.

PATSY. (*Alarmed, goes to bathroom and opens door.*) Say——

ERWIN. Huh!

PATSY. Oh, excuse me—say, how long does it take you to dope 'em out? (ERWIN *mumbles.*) O. K. (*Shuts door and turns to others triumphantly. Sits armchair.*) About an hour. We got plenty of time.

FRANKIE. (There's some good races, too.

CHARLIE. (*Sits.*) If he can only pick 'em like yesterday.

(MABEL *enters.*)

MABEL. Hello. I didn't think you'd be up so early, Pats.

PATSY. Hello, sugar.

MABEL. (*Sits on bed.*) Where's the boy friend?

FRANKIE. Gettin' dressed——

PATSY. (*Finding a verse on chair under him.*) Say, here's another one of them verses. (*Reads it.*) Listen, fellows, do you know we're associatin' with a genius?

MABEL. What's that?

PATSY. Poetry. Erwin's poetry.

MABEL. Oh, gee, I thought he was a guy who fixed horse races.

PATSY. He does. He just does poetry for a hobby.

FRANKIE. (*Picking up verses.*) Yeah, I better get those around for him. Room 909 he said. We don't want him to lose his job. (*He goes to desk.*)

PATSY. You know, I feel sorry for that guy. Slavin' every day. Doin' the same things over and over.

FRANKIE. I can't find a big envelope. (*Looking through desk.*)

CHARLIE. (*At desk.*) They have 'em downstairs.

PATSY. Listen to this:

"Why was it that I chose to roam
Cross Land and Sea so far from home?
If that be Life—My Mother Dear,
I send this card of Love and Cheer."

Mother's Day No. 37. That touches you—you know that—right here.

MABEL. Yeah . . . like when you're seein' a good sad movie . . . geez ——

PATSY. You know, this Erwin guy ain't bein' appreciated.

CHARLIE. (*Sits at head of bed.*) You mean he's better than he is?

PATSY. I mean he's better than forty bucks . . . do you know any other guys who could sit down and write them gems for forty bucks a week?

FRANKIE. Well, I guess there is some guys . . .

PATSY. You don't know any off hand?

FRANKIE. No.

PATSY. That's just it. We ought to do somethin'.

MABEL. Like what?

PATSY. Like somethin', anyway. It gets me sore to think a nice guy like him is workin' for a guy like this here fellow he's tellin' about all the time—J. G. Carver. Look up the Holly Cheer Greeting Company. I don't know Mr. Carver, but he's probably a louse. . . .

CHARLIE. (FRANKIE *looks in phone book.*) What are you goin' to do, anyways?

PATSY. I'm goin' to get Erwin a raise. I feel for him like my own brother. That's the trouble with people in this world—they get a good thing like him and they take advantage of it.

FRANKIE. Give me Bogardus 4–6752. . . . I'll get it for you.

PATSY. (*Crossing and taking phone.*) Let me have it. Let me talk to him. . . . Mr. Carver. . . . Just tell him it's important. . . . Hello, Carver. . . . This is a very good friend of Mr. Erwin Trowbridge . . . in fact, I'm his manager. . . . Since yesterday. . . . Oh, they're all written. . . . They're gems. . . . That's what they are. . . . Well, before I sent them around I thought we'd discuss terms. Those verses are the best verses I ever read and I've read a lot of verses. . . . What I thought was this . . . we might as well talk man to man . . . you're gettin' away with murder. Forty bucks a week. . . . Yeah. . . . Yeah. . . . That's what I call a steal. I'll

bet you couldn't —— Hello . . . hello. . . . He hung up. . . . Is that polite? Is that the way to talk to me that's manager of a poet practically?
CHARLIE. Maybe one of us should go down and punch him in the nose.
FRANKIE. (*Stopping* CHARLIE.) No—let's not start any fights . . . not till we make some money.
PATSY. I don't like that guy. (*Sits armchair.*) It ain't what he said to me, you understand, but he said for Erwin to go to hell too.
FRANKIE. (*Sits at desk.*) It looks like Erwin stayed up all night for nothin'.
PATSY. Like hell he has. The world should see art like that . . . those gems should be put in barrooms . . . railroad stations . . . on calendars . . . wait, I got it.
FRANKIE. We ought to have somethin' because if Erwin finds out I haven't taken ——
PATSY. Liebowitz!
MABEL. The printer.
PATSY. Jake Liebowitz, who did all the classy postal cards for that smoker last month.
FRANKIE. He prints lots of stuff.
PATSY. Suppose it cost us a hundred bucks . . . get a couple o' guys to go around sell 'em to factories, clubs, the Y. M. C. A. . . . the Y. W. C. A. . . . the Y. M. H. A. and all the railroad stations then . . . railroad stations! (*Picks up phone.*) Frankie, have you ever been in a washroom in a railroad station?
FRANKIE. Sure. Haven't you?
PATSY. Lots of times. Well in those railroad stations . . . not only railroads, but all over . . . you've seen those verses like: "A man's ambition must be small to write his name . . ." (*At phone.*) Kitty . . . Patsy . . . tell Moses to come right up here and bring a big envelope. (*Hangs up.*)
MABEL. . . . and the one about sittin' and thinkin'.
PATSY. Sure. Well nobody's thought to commercialize that kind of poetry . . . they're gems. That's what that guy can do. If he can write serious stuff like he has here, he can write funny stuff too.
FRANKIE. Gee, that's a swell idea.
CHARLIE. Come in.

(*Enter* MOSES.)

FRANKIE. I'll bet he never thought of that.

MOSES. (*Holding envelope.*) This all right, Mr. Patsy?
PATSY. Yeah. That's what I want.
FRANKIE. Here, give it to me.
PATSY. (*Tossing coin.*) Here you are, Moses. Frankie, take those around to Jake Liebowitz. I'll call him and tell him you're coming.
FRANKIE. O. K. I'll shoot right over. (*Exit up* L.)
PATSY. Come around later and I'll give you a horse. Penn. 6–7811.
MOSES. If it's all the same to you, Mr. Patsy, I'd sooner have a number.
PATSY. Mr. Erwin only has horses.
MOSES. All right then, I guess I'll have to take a horse. (*Exit.*)
PATSY. (*In phone.*) Hello . . . Jake? This is Patsy. How are you? . . . Well, say listen, you ain't so busy . . . yeah, I know . . . but listen, I want a special job done on verses . . . no, not singin' verses . . . poetry verses . . . you know—"Roses are Red" . . . yeah . . . about a thousand and, Jake, I want them on shiny paper, with lace maybe. They'll be there in a couple of minutes. Don't leave before you get them. O. K. (*Hangs up.*)
MABEL. If you're going to do all this, what's Erwin going to get out of it?
PATSY. All of it . . . we're only helping him out.
MABEL. Oh, like bein' in business for himself, huh?
PATSY. Sure. All he has to do is write 'em. When it gets going good . . . he just stays home and picks horses and the verses sell themselves . . . because they're good.
MABEL. That's what I call givin' him a break.
ERWIN. (*Enters and sees* MABEL.) Oh, good morning.
MABEL. Hello. I hope you feel better than yesterday.
ERWIN. Well, I guess I do. Maybe I ought to go out and get a little breakfast. (*Coming down to bureau.*)
PATSY. Say, Erwin, I was just talking to Mr. Carver on the phone.
ERWIN. You were?
PATSY. Yeah. I don't think that he likes you so much. I could tell by his voice.
ERWIN. Why, what's happened?
PATSY. Somethin' good . . . we're settin' you up in business on your own.
ERWIN. But what about Mr. Carver?
PATSY. To hell with him. He don't appreciate you.
ERWIN. Doesn't he like my verses?
PATSY. I told him I wouldn't even let him see them.

ERWIN. Why not? What right have you to do a thing like that? I'll lose my job. Where are my verses? (*Rushing past* PATSY.)

PATSY. (*Holding him.*) Wait a minute, Erwin, this is for your good. . . .

ERWIN. Where are my verses?

PATSY. Listen, Erwin, we sent them over to Liebowitz. . . .

ERWIN. Who is Liebowitch?

PATSY. He's one of our best friends. He's going to print your verses so they'll be sold all over the country. See?

ERWIN. Please don't. You can't do this to me . . . you fellows might think this is funny, but I'm going to lose my job . . . you don't know what it means to have a job, fifty-two weeks in the year —forty dollars a week. . . . (*As he says this he sits on corner of bed.*)

PATSY. (*Going to him.*) Don't you know you rate more than that? Don't you know that big crook is cheating hell out of you? Here you are starving along on forty a week, while that big piece of salami is living high with swell offices in the Wedgewood Building. Sure. And he made it all off you. Now Liebowitz is going to print your verses so that every home . . .

ERWIN. I don't want Liebowitz to print my verses. All I want is to work for Mr. Carver.

PATSY. But he's a louse.

ERWIN. (*Jumping up.*) He is not. Don't you say that about Mr. Carver . . . he's the only boss I ever had and I like to work for him. Get me back my verses.

(FRANKIE *enters.*)

FRANKIE. Well, everything's O. K.

PATSY. Frankie, you've got to get those verses back.

FRANKIE. What the hell is this?

PATSY. You're careless, that's all.

FRANKIE. I can't get 'em back now.

ERWIN. What's happened to my verses?

FRANKIE. Nothing's happened to them. Liebowitz was waitin' for me at the door when I got there and he said, "Congratulate me, Frankie, my daughter is having a baby at the Beth Israel Hospital and my son is being confirmed at the synagogue" . . . so I congratulated him and he took the verses with him in a taxicab. Say, it's gettin' late; don't you think Erwin ought to start pickin' the horses?

ERWIN. Horses? . . . I can't even think of horses.

PATSY. (*Crossing to* FRANKIE *and giving him a push.*) Erwin can't pick any horses until he gets the verses back.

FRANKIE. Well, what the hell are we going to do about it?

PATSY. We gotta do something. We gotta get 'em back.

ERWIN. Working hard all my life . . . trying to get some place, trying to build a reputation. (*Sinking into chair.*)

MABEL. (*Rises.*) Don't you worry, Erwin. It'll be all right. Boys, you got to find Liebowitz . . . it's a cinch he's in one of two places; his daughter is havin' a baby at the Beth Israel Hospital and his son is being confirmed at the synagogue.

FRANKIE. But suppose he's gone to his home? He said he had to get dressed.

PATSY. I'll take care of that. Mabel is right. We got to find him. We got to keep Erwin happy so his mind can work good and pick the horses. Frankie, you go to the Beth Israel Hospital. And Charlie, you look for him in the synagogue. Come on, boys, get moving . . . and don't forget the name, Frankie, Beth Israel.

CHARLIE. Why should I have to go to the synagogue? All right. If you say so that makes it right. (*Exit.*)

FRANKIE. Beth Israel. . . . Beth Israel. . . . (*Exit up* L.)

PATSY. There now . . . we'll get the verses right back, see, Erwin? . . . Wait till I look up where he lives.

MABEL. You see, Erwin, now there isn't anything to worry about. (*Shaking* ERWIN.) Erwin —— Say, look, Patsy . . . he's all pale . . . Erwin. . . . I think he's fainted or something.

PATSY. Fainted, geez.

MABEL. Should I phone down for a doctor?

PATSY. Doctor? No! Give me a hand. Put him on the bed. We don't want any doctors around. (*They take him over to the bed.*) We'll get him a drink—a couple o' drinks will fix him up. (*Goes to phone.*)

MABEL. Maybe that's all he needs—just a pick-me-up.

PATSY. (*In phone.*) Hello—get me the bar.

(ERWIN *opens eyes for a moment.*)

MABEL. Oh, Patsy,—he just opened his eyes.

PATSY. Say, his health is important now—remember that—we got to take good care of him.

MABEL. You bet ——

PATSY. (*In phone.*) Hello, Harry—Patsy. Are you very busy? Well, bring up a bottle of rye right away. Yeah. (*Hangs up. Picks up phone book.*)

MABEL. (*To* ERWIN.) How do you feel now? (ERWIN *nods.*) Sure —sure, just a teensie weensie hangover, that's all.

PATSY. Sure, he'll be all right.—Geez, there's about a million Liebowitzes — Abraham — Benjamin — David — Herman — Isaac — Jacob —— (*Picks up receiver.*) Chelsea 3-1098.

HARRY. (*Enters.*) You sounded like you was in a hurry. (*Looks at* ERWIN.) Geez, ain't he come to yet?

PATSY. Yeah, but he passed out again.

MABEL. He's about half to, now—but I'm makin' him rest.

HARRY. Do you think he can stand another drink?

PATSY. Sure, that's just what —— Hello, Jake ——

HARRY. (*To* MABEL.) Got a corkscrew?

MABEL. Yeah. (*Goes into bathroom and comes out during following speech with corkscrew.*)

PATSY. Jake, I gotta have those verses back—never mind why.—Oh—well, how long you goin' to be there?—The hell with the baby. This is a matter of life and death.—I'll be right over for them. —Wait for me. (*Hangs up; grabs hat.*) Work on him, Harry—he's got to pick those horses. Mabel, don't let Erwin get out of here and don't let him call anybody up till I get back. (PATSY *exits.*)

(HARRY *pours drink.*)

MABEL. (*Bringing another glass from bathroom.*) Pour me one, too, Harry. I feel kind of faint myself. (HARRY *pours one for* MABEL.) I never seen so much excitement. (*Drinks it down.*)

HARRY. I wish he'd hurry up and come to. I want another horse today. (ERWIN *groans.*) Here, drink this. (*Forces drink down* ERWIN'S *throat.*)

ERWIN. Oh—Audrey! Gosh! (*Sits up.*)

HARRY. Now, how do you feel?

ERWIN. (*Rises.*) I don't know.

HARRY. Better get him under the covers. Get his pants off.

ERWIN. (*Alarmed.*) What?

MABEL. (*Going to* ERWIN.) Sure. (*Starts to unbutton his pants.*)

ERWIN. Hey, don't—no, no, no. Please.

MABEL. What's the matter?

ERWIN. It tickles.

HARRY. Better let me do it. (*Pulls his pants off—puts* ERWIN *in bed. Phone rings.*)

ERWIN. I'm all right.

HARRY. Sure you are.

MABEL. (*Answering phone.*) Hello . . . yeah . . . he's here—well he just got here—he's helpin' me—he's—all right—I'll tell him. (*Hangs up.*) You got some customers at the bar, Harry—you better go down.

HARRY. (*Tucking* ERWIN *in.*) Who was that?

MABEL. Mac.

HARRY. Ah—nuts to him. (*To* ERWIN.) What do you think of Mad Hatter in the first race today, Erwin?

ERWIN. I don't know.

HARRY. Well, take your time. But don't forget me, will you?—And if there's any little thing I can do for you, you let me know.

MABEL. You better hop down there or Mac'll be yappin' some more.

(MABEL *crosses to dresser, gets drink, crosses up to bed.*)

HARRY. That damn bar—it's a nuisance. (*Exits.*)

(ERWIN *groans.*)

MABEL. (*Crossing with drink.*) Here, Erwin, now don't excite yourself. Gee, it's awful nice of you to stay here and help Patsy like you been doin'. (*She sits and drinks.*)

ERWIN. I was desperate or I wouldn't have done such a thing.

MABEL. But if you knew how much we liked to have you here—I don't mean just the boys, I mean more particularly just myself personally.

ERWIN. Give me back my pants.

MABEL. What's the matter?

ERWIN. I ought to call up my wife.

MABEL. Not just now, Erwin—I don't want you to get out of bed. You might faint again.

ERWIN. I ought to call her. I've punished her enough. She'll be worried.

MABEL. But listen now, pet, just wait till Patsy gets back, will you? 'Cause I promised him I wouldn't let you call anybody.

ERWIN. Yes, but I haven't been home all night.

MABEL. She must be used to that.

ERWIN. Oh, no, she isn't.

MABEL. You're a good deal different than most men then. God knows Patsy's liable to disappear for a week at a time. But he's awfully good to me though.—You ought to see all the swell things he gave me when I quit the Follies for him! . . . Two weeks later they tried a four-horse parlay at Saratoga and we lost everything.—I didn't have a nightgown left to my name.

ERWIN. Oh! That must have been terrible.

MABEL. Well, it's just the breaks. Now, it looks as though things is brightening up again since you come into my life.

ERWIN. Where's my pencil—quick —— (*He writes.*)

MABEL. What is it? You got the first race? (ERWIN *shakes his head. Gets pencil and paper off bed.*) Let's see. (*She takes the paper on bureau and reads.*)

"My soul was sad as darkest night.
But now the world seems fair and bright
Because you came so true and fine.
Oh, stay and be my Valentine."

ERWIN. Valentine's Day No. 1. It doesn't do any hurt to get ahead of schedule.

MABEL. Yeah. If you're ahead then you're a fast worker, is that it?

ERWIN. What?

MABEL. Never mind. (*Reads.*) Stay and be my Valentine. Gee, that's wonderful! . . . I'm crazy about poetry.

ERWIN. I don't get much time to write real poetry. I've been so busy with my Mother's Day verses.

MABEL. Oh . . . gee, I haven't heard from Mom in a long time—of course I ain't written to her lately—maybe I ought to send her one of them . . . a verse . . . it might make her feel good . . . you see, I ain't sure she's my mother. (*Drinks.*)

ERWIN. Oh, but she'd feel good anyway.

MABEL. I guess so. I haven't seen her since I came to New York to go on the stage.

ERWIN. Did you really used to be on the stage?

MABEL. Yeah, I used to be in the Follies once. I'd like to get back in show business but Patsy doesn't think I look as good as I used to. (*Stands up and pats her hips.*) Don't you think I could get back if I worked hard?

ERWIN. Sure, I'll bet you could. Of course I've never seen a Follies girl close to before—only from the balcony. You look all right to me.

MABEL. Do I really, Erwin?

ERWIN. Why yes—yes—you're beautiful.

MABEL. Gee, I like you . . . (*Sits on bed.*) just think—maybe I have read one of your poems in a magazine—like a movie magazine—and here I am sittin' talking to you. . . . I guess that's what you call romantic, huh? Gee, I'm pretty jealous of your wife, you know it?

ERWIN. You are? Why?

MABEL. Havin' you all to herself—I'm just thinkin' how wonderful it would be to travel around the world with you—listenin' to your poetry and helpin' you make a lot of money bettin' on the horses.

ERWIN. Oh, but I wouldn't bet—that would spoil it all.

MABEL. Well, I mean—just enough for a fur coat and stuff like that.

ERWIN. But I don't think I could tell what ones are going to win if I ever started betting on them.

MABEL. Well, anyhow, you could make a lot of money if you wanted to just with words for songs like they have in shows. You know, lyrics?

ERWIN. You think so?

MABEL. Sure. Say, lots of times I sang words in the chorus that wasn't half as good as that.

ERWIN. Did you sing in the Follies?

MABEL. Yeah—I did a specialty once. Ya want to see it? (*He nods.*) Say, I'd do anything for you. (*Goes to radio.*) 'Cause I'm crazy about poetry, that's why. (*Turns radio on. Music. Tries a few steps.*) I may not be so good till I get limbered up. I can't do a thing with this dress on—I guess among friends it's all right, huh?

ERWIN. What is? (MABEL *starts to take off dress. Radio begins to talk—on laugh.* ANNOUNCER—*"Two tablets daily and assure yourself a perfect health and a happy old age. At this time we present Ivan Aronson and his jazzy cossacks in a program of dance music.—Take it away, Ivan!" Music.*) I think—I ought to telephone my wife——

MABEL. Don't you want to see my dance?

ERWIN. Yes, I do.

MABEL. (*Gets music.*) Here we go. Now, you're the audience. I come out, you see, with a big spot on me. (*Dances.*) The other girls are jealous 'cause I got a specialty —— (*She kicks, exposing all.*) Of course this is just a rough idea ——

ERWIN. (*As she kicks.*) Say, that's good!

MABEL. This is my finish. (*She whirls across stage, staggers and turns off radio.*)

ERWIN. What's the matter?

MABEL. (*Breathless.*) Out of practice . . . haven't done this for so long . . . got dizzy.
ERWIN. I'll give you a drink. (*Pours drink.*)

(PATSY *enters while* ERWIN *is giving* MABEL *a drink. He stands at door and looks. He has verses in his hand.*)

PATSY. What the hell's this?
ERWIN. Have you got my verses?
PATSY. Yeah . . .
ERWIN. She was doin' a dance—and all of a sudden—she got dizzy.
PATSY. Oh yeah?
ERWIN. Yes.

(PATSY *walks slowly toward* MABEL.)

PATSY. You get your dress on and go back to your room.
MABEL. What's the matter, Patsy? (*Gets dress.*)
PATSY. I said get your dress on and go back to your room.
MABEL. He wanted to phone his wife and ——
PATSY. All right, never mind the lip—get back to your room. (MABEL *backs up to door.*) You're just good and lucky I don't take a poke at you. Go on.
MABEL. But, Patsy ——
PATSY. Get out. Get out before I kick your teeth in—you crooked little punk.
MABEL. Geez, you never talked to me like this before. (*She goes out almost in tears, carrying dress.*)
ERWIN. I hope you don't think —— (PATSY *tears verses.*) Hey, stop that ——
PATSY. Get those on and take yourself out of here.
ERWIN. Hey, my verses!
PATSY. (*Throws pants at him.*) Get your pants on and get out of here before I lose my temper . . . you double-crossin' little . . .
ERWIN. My verses! (*Goes to bathroom; locks door.*)

(PATSY, *in a rage, tears verses some more.* CHARLIE *and* FRANKIE *enter together.*)

CHARLIE. Hey, what the hell did you do to Mabel? She's cryin' in the hall.
FRANKIE. Geez, I never seen a girl cry so much.
PATSY. I didn't do a thing to her, but I should have. (*Points toward bathroom, keeps one verse to tear.*) Can you imagine!

FRANKIE. What?
PATSY. And me thinkin' he was a sap.
CHARLIE. Well, what's happened?
PATSY. What the hell do you think?
FRANKIE. (*Crosses to* C.) She said she was just tryin' to be nice to him till you got back.
PATSY. Yeah. Nice is right. Took three weeks and a diamond bracelet to get her that nice to me.
CHARLIE. Well, you told her to hold him, didn't you?
FRANKIE. Yeah—maybe she didn't like it no better than you did. Maybe she just seen her duty, that's all.
PATSY. Aw—it's my fault, I suppose, for leavin' them alone together.
CHARLIE. No, but you can trust Mabel—geez, I never could get nowhere with her ——
PATSY. What?
CHARLIE. I mean—if I'd tried. No, you just mistook the looks of things.
FRANKIE. Where's Erwin?
PATSY. In there.
CHARLIE. What didja do to him?
PATSY. I told him to get dressed and get the hell out of here.
FRANKIE. He ain't gone yet, is he?
PATSY. No. But he will as soon as he gets dressed.
CHARLIE. How about the horses for today?
PATSY. We'll select our own.
CHARLIE. (*Closes in.*) And lose our shirts! Now listen, wise guy, he's just as much ours as he is yours.
FRANKIE. That's what I say. You can't throw him out—just because you think your girl happened to go for him. And you ain't even sure—you couldn't prove it in a court of law.
PATSY. How would you feel if your girl happened to do that?
FRANKIE. To do what?—how do you know she did anything?—and suppose she did—what I mean is—well, gee—you know, a guy like Erwin. That wouldn't be much of anything.
CHARLIE. Sure.—Gee, you don't mean to tell me you're worried about a guy like him.
PATSY. Worried? What's that got to do with it? God! there's such a thing like decency, ain't there? It don't look right to me to come back and find some guy in his underpants passin' my girl drinks—it don't look right.

CHARLIE. She was just stallin' for time.

(PATSY *paces back and forth.*)

FRANKIE. Sure, she was just trying to keep him from phoning his wife. Geez, she was willin' to come through for you and you don't even appreciate it. Ain't that the kind of a girl you want—ain't that loyalty, huh?
CHARLIE. What more do you want? She's always played ball with you.
PATSY. (*Stopping.*) Yeah—but ——
CHARLIE. What more do you want? She's only tryin' to keep this guy on the fire so's you can make enough money to buy a house and settle down with her.
PATSY. Yeah?
CHARLIE. That's what she said.
FRANKIE. And besides, Harry helped take his pants off, you know that, don't you?
PATSY. No.
CHARLIE. Sure. That don't sound very sensual to me.
FRANKIE. You sap. You ought to be busted right in the nose for makin' her cry that way.
PATSY. Was she really cryin'?
CHARLIE. Was she cryin' —— Geez!

(PATSY *goes right to phone.*)

PATSY. (*Picking up phone.*) Hello—give me Mabel's room . . .

(FRANKIE *takes drink.* CHARLIE *sees verses on floor, picks them up.*)

CHARLIE. What the hell happened to the verses?
PATSY. Oh, I got sore . . . hello, Mabel . . . now listen, honey, stop crying . . . well, I didn't mean it—but I couldn't help it—you know how I feel about you . . . I just didn't like the looks of things . . . well, it did look bad to me when I come in . . . now listen, I want you to dry your eyes and forget all about it . . . yeah . . . I'll tell you what I want you to do . . . put on that pretty dress I bought you yesterday and go out and look at apartments . . . all right, look at a house, what the hell do I care. . . . Papa wouldn't treat you that way, it's just 'cause papa loves you.
CHARLIE. Papa gives me a pain in the —— Hang up, will you? You said enough.
PATSY. (*Hangs up.*) Gee, she *was* cryin'.

FRANKIE. Listen, boys, quit foolin' around about women and all that sort of tripe—let's get down to something important—now, how about those horses?
CHARLIE. Yeah, it's after one o'clock.
PATSY. Aw, it only takes him about an hour.
CHARLIE. Well, we ought to get him started.

(*Bathroom door opens.* ERWIN *enters. Starts to put on coat which has been on back of chair* R.)

FRANKIE. Hey, where you goin'?
ERWIN. I'm goin' to the office.
FRANKIE. (*Going to him. Shocked.*) Oh, you wouldn't do a thing like that!
ERWIN. (*Passing* FRANKIE.) Where's my verses?
CHARLIE. (*Stops him.*) No, but wait a minute—let's talk it over, that's all.
ERWIN. I haven't time.
PATSY. Now, listen, Erwin, I'm sorry I spoke to you the way I did. It did look a little bad—but I'm goin' to square everything. I've just been talking to Mabel.
ERWIN. You ought to be ashamed of yourself. She's too good for you.
PATSY. It's all right, pal, it's all right—only I just forgot myself.
ERWIN. Where'd you put my verses?
CHARLIE. After all, Erwin, you got nothing against Frankie and me.
ERWIN. No, no, I haven't, but ——
FRANKIE. Geez, we nursed you back to health and everything like you was a baby almost ——
PATSY. You wouldn't walk out on us after the way we took care of you. (*Takes him by lapels.*) Listen, Erwin, didn't you ever lose your temper?
ERWIN. Yes, I did.
PATSY. Well, that's me—and I'm sorry. If you walk out on us now the boys will hold it against me for the rest of my life. They'll say I insulted you and that's why you left us.
ERWIN. I have to get to the office. I'm late now. And Mr. Carver is going to be upset. Maybe he won't even give me my job back after the way you talked to him ——
PATSY. (*Tough.*) He'll give it to you, if I have to go down and ——
CHARLIE. Nix, nix.

PATSY. We'll buy the joint and let you run it.
ERWIN. I don't want to run it—I just want to work for Mr. Carver. Anyhow, I have to go and explain to him.
CHARLIE. Couldn't you just dope out the horses before you go?
ERWIN. No.
FRANKIE. I'm disappointed in you, Erwin. I thought we could trust you. I certainly did.
ERWIN. (*Worried.*) Well, I'd like to help you. . . .
PATSY. (*Acting the martyr while others gesture encouragement.*) It's all right, only, Erwin—I must give you your ten per cent before you go. (*Counts out money.*)
ERWIN. What? Well—I—
PATSY. If you feel like letting us down I wouldn't want to be the one to interfere. (*Passes money.*) Here you are. One hundred and twelve bucks! Sorry it ain't more, but I thought we was going to have longer to work on it. Might have got up into some real coin if you would have stayed with us today.
CHARLIE. Yes, I guess your share today would have been a thousand dollars or so.
FRANKIE. Yeah—it's too bad.

(*Knock on door.*)

PATSY. (*Tough.*) Who is it?

(MABEL *sticks head in door.*)

MABEL. Did you say come in?
PATSY. (*Sweet loud kiss.*) Oh, come in, honey. (*She enters in new dress.*) You're just in time to say good-bye to Erwin.
MABEL. Good-bye?
PATSY. He thinks I didn't treat you right, so he's walking out on us.
MABEL. Aw.
ERWIN. I'd like to stay, honest, I would, I feel terrible about it, but ——
MABEL. Oh, Erwin, I can't bear to have you go.
FRANKIE. If you'd just dope out a couple of horses before you go.
PATSY. I tell you what, Erwin; here's the solution to the whole proposition: you can't take these verses back to the office like this, they're all torn—you just sit down and wait a few minutes while we copy 'em for you.
ERWIN. Well ——

CHARLIE. (*Picks up verses and sits on bed.*) Sure, we'll do it—then we can all part the best of friends.

FRANKIE. Sure—move over—give me a couple of those.

PATSY. And while you're waiting for us to do it you can just pass the time figuring a couple of horses.

ERWIN. I can help copy verses.

PATSY. No, no, we tore 'em up; we'll copy 'em. You figure horses.—Give me some of those, will you?—You figure horses. Give him a pencil, Mabel.

MABEL. (*Giving him pencil and racing paper from desk.*) Sure. Here's a pencil—Erwin. And there's the racing form.

ERWIN. Well, all right—I'll try.

MABEL. I knew you would—now—sit right here.

PATSY. That's the boy.

CHARLIE. I always said he was a regular fellow.

PATSY. You bet, you can count on Erwin.

MABEL. Oh yeah, he'll come through all right.

CHARLIE. Good old Erwin!

FRANKIE. (*Topping them.*) All right, boys, don't talk so much. Let him concentrate.

(ERWIN *thinks, then crosses legs.*)

MABEL. Is there anything I can do?

CHARLIE. Yeah, go into your dance.

PATSY. Shut up.

CHARLIE. Well, don't be talking so much and bustin' up his thoughts.

PATSY. Well, who's talkin'?—You are.

MABEL. Yeah, he's doin' all the ——

FRANKIE. Shut up, all of you.

CHARLIE. Come on now, let's not argue so much; get busy on Erwin's verses.

(ERWIN *tears off slip of paper, looks at it, shakes head and stuffs paper under pillow.*)

FRANKIE. Sure. (ERWIN *writes on new sheet of paper.*) No good, huh, Erwin?

PATSY. Leave him alone. Leave him alone.

FRANKIE. No but he wrote one down. He put it under the pillow.

ERWIN. It isn't anything. It's no good.

CHARLIE. (*Reaching under pillow and reading paper.*) Equipoise.

PATSY. Equipoise. Runs in the fourth, huh?
FRANKIE. Equipoise. That's the one I was going to pick.
ERWIN. But it doesn't count, I tell you.

(*They all rise.*)

CHARLIE. Why don't it?
ERWIN. I don't know.
CHARLIE. You mean it's no good?
ERWIN. No!
CHARLIE. He ain't going to come through—I can feel it.
PATSY. (*Going to* ERWIN.) He is so. You wouldn't let me down, would you, Erwin?
ERWIN. (*Rising and throwing down pencil and paper.*) It's no use.
PATSY. What do you mean it's no use? Now, Erwin, you ain't going to get discouraged?
ERWIN. I can't figure them out just sitting here. I've always done them on a bus.
CHARLIE. Well, just imagine you're on a bus.
PATSY. Geez, no wonder he couldn't think of 'em sittin' there on that lousy bed—(*Rushing him to chair by window.*) come over here by the window, Erwin. This is more like a bus. Slip that chair under him, Frankie. Give him that pencil and paper. Just try—just concentrate. Now, just pretend you're on the bus, see? Just concentrate. (ERWIN *concentrates. They watch him.* CHARLIE *is in rear of* ERWIN.)

CHARLIE. (*Gently, to give atmosphere but not to break spell.*) Fares, please—have your fares ready ——

(PATSY *wants to swing on him.* ERWIN *jumps up.*)

ERWIN. It's no use. I can't do it.
PATSY. But you don't try, Erwin.
ERWIN. I've tried before. I'm not kidding. They only come to me on a bus.
CHARLIE. Would a taxi do? A nice taxi with a radio?
ERWIN. No.
PATSY. Hell, a taxi is better than a bus any time. And we can get one quicker.
ERWIN. (*Shakes head, crosses to* C. *below bed.*) Only on a bus.
PATSY. (*Reaching in pocket for money.*) All right. Frankie, go downstairs and reserve the rear seat of the Coney Island bus. Tell

them to throw out all them stooges. Get the best lookin' bus you can.

ERWIN. Now, wait a minute. . . . I hope you're not going to think I'm awfully particular—but you see, I couldn't do them on the Coney Island bus.

PATSY. For God's sake—why not?

ERWIN. Because I've always done them on the bus that goes to Ozone Heights.

CHARLIE. Where do you get one of them?

PATSY. (*Annoyed.*) No—no ——

FRANKIE. We could just change the sign.

PATSY. (*Yelling.*) No—no—no ——

MABEL. If you fellows would let him do it his own way ——

PATSY. Yeh, that's what we're going to do. Now shut up!

ERWIN. Why —— (*Looks up at them, shocked by sharp tone.*)

PATSY. (*Almost fatherly.*) Well, ain't that right—they're getting you flustered, ain't they, kid?

ERWIN. I am getting kind of mixed up. You see, usually, just for fun, I figure them out going home.

PATSY. All right—that's easy—now you'd like to go home, wouldn't you?

ERWIN. Yes, I would.

PATSY. All right, that's what you're going to do.

CHARLIE. (*Walking away. Sotto voce.*) Good-bye, we'll never see him again.

PATSY. You're going out and get on your regular bus just like you always do. Mabel and Frankie they'll go with you. We'll be copying verses—but in the meantime—you'll be taking a nice ride and then you can drop in and see the wife . . . tell her everything is fine.

ERWIN. Yes, I'd like to do that.

PATSY. But just before you tell her, see, phone us what horses to bet on. We'll be right here copying your verses and waiting for the dope.

ERWIN. All right. Let's get started. Come on, Frankie ——

CHARLIE. And Erwin, no looking out of windows—just horses.

PATSY. Unless you hurry we ain't going to make the first race as it is.

ERWIN. Where's my necktie?

CHARLIE. You never had none.

FRANKIE. Take mine.

PATSY. Keep it on. I got plenty. (*Takes ties from bureau drawer—throws on bed.*) Help yourself.

ERWIN. (*Selects a loud tie and puts it on.*) Oh, thanks.
PATSY. Frankie, take the *Telegraph.*
FRANKIE. Where the hell is it?
MABEL. Here it is on the bed. Erwin was sittin' on it.
PATSY. Have you got a pencil, Erwin?
CHARLIE. Have you got your little black book?
PATSY. Yeah!
FRANKIE. I've got it right here.
PATSY. Stick it in his pocket.

(FRANKIE *does so.*)

ERWIN. I'll bet my wife will be surprised when she sees this necktie.
PATSY. Get going. Get going.
ERWIN. Where's my hat?
CHARLIE. Here you are ——
FRANKIE. (*Goes to dresser, gets hat.*) I'll get it for you. Ring for the elevator, Mabel.
MABEL. (*They rush him out.*) All right, but hurry.
ERWIN. Seems as if I'd been away forever.
PATSY. Get on the right bus, Erwin.
CHARLIE. Treat him nice. Buy him a soda.

CURTAIN

ACT III

SCENE 1: *Ozone Heights.*
Orchestra plays "It's the Talk of the Town."
AT RISE: GLORIA *and* AL *are seen through window* R. *passing the house. The room is littered with newspapers.* CLARENCE *is peeking out windows. He jumps to another window to watch someone outside.* AUDREY *comes downstairs in a new dress.*

CLARENCE. They took a picture of the house. (AUDREY, *dry-eyed and repressed, walks across room and sits.*) Wouldn't it be wonderful if they'd put that in the paper? (*Points to paper on floor.*) That *Newark Star* gave us a very bad write-up. . . . Nothing about Dobbins Drive . . . just said a versifier of Ozone Heights is missing. (*Notices* AUDREY.) You didn't need to get all dressed up—she said she'd take your picture just as you were.
AUDREY. I got dressed up for Mr. Carver, not for her. I'm sure that Erwin would want me to look as well as I can.
CLARENCE. Well, from time to time I've said things against J. G. Carver, but I take 'em all back. His heart is in the right place or he wouldn't be coming out here. Gee, I wonder if I could interest him in a house.
AUDREY. He isn't coming out here about houses, he's coming out about Erwin.
CLARENCE. Well, if I've got to support you the rest of my life, the least I can get out of this is maybe a sale or two. (*Snaps fingers and sits.*) Or a tip on a horse. Doggone, if Erwin was going to walk out that way he could at least have left a *hot tip.* He's probably out at some bookie's right now putting his money on the winners.—Gosh, what wouldn't I give to know which ones!
AUDREY. You don't have to support me the rest of your life, so don't say that again. And if you must keep on making remarks that Erwin has run away, then I'll have to ask you not to come in my house any more.
CLARENCE. Why, Sis.

(*Front door opens and* GLORIA GRAY *enters, followed by* AL, *the photographer.*)

GLORIA. (*Pointing to davenport.*) Now, Mrs. Trowbridge, if you'll just stand over here, please. Have you got a handkerchief?

AUDREY. (*At davenport.*) Handkerchief?

GLORIA. Yes, you ought to be crying, you know ——

AUDREY. I'm not going to cry any more. . . .

CLARENCE. She cried terrible this morning. But she's a brave little woman.

GLORIA. Brave little woman. There's a very trenchant phrase—remind me to use that, will you, Al?

CLARENCE. (GLORIA *gives him a cold smile.*) Want me in the picture?

AL. Still —— (*Snaps picture.*)

GLORIA. That's fine. Now I'd like just one more. We'll take another one brave. That's just as good. (*To* CLARENCE.) You're the brother of the missing man, are you?

CLARENCE. No, I'm the brother of the wife of the missing man, and I'm the owner of this row of houses here.

GLORIA. They're very attractive.

CLARENCE. They're all alike.

GLORIA. I noticed that.

AL. Still ——

GLORIA. All right, Al, you might shoot him just for luck.

CLARENCE. Let's see where'll we a —— (*Picks up chair and looks for a spot to place it and sit for picture.*)

AL. (*Snapping picture of* CLARENCE'S *rear.*) Still ——

CLARENCE. (*Still holding chair.*) Oh, I wasn't ready.

GLORIA. That's all right—you looked worried—just the right expression.

CLARENCE. I am worried—he was a fine fellow ——

AUDREY. (*Taking photo from phone table.*) Now, here's the picture of Erwin—I hate to part with it.—It's the only one I've got ——

GLORIA. Oh, we'll send it back in good condition —— (*Writes on face.*) Here you are, Al —— (*Tosses it to* AL.)

AUDREY. But of course, if it'll help to find Erwin . . .

GLORIA. Sure it will. Somebody might recognize him—and—you'll get a lot of people who think they do. I'll promise you that ——

CLARENCE. If you'd print a description I should think it might help. When he left here he was wearing a gray suit, brown hat, black shoes . . .

AUDREY. And no necktie.

GLORIA. No necktie —— (AUDREY *shakes head.*) Why was that?
AUDREY. He was in a hurry. He was late.
GLORIA. Often do that, does he?
AUDREY. (*Shakes head.*) No—it's the first time.
GLORIA. And—this is the first time he ever stayed away from home overnight? (AUDREY *nods.*) And the first time he ever went to work without a necktie?
AL. Doesn't look like a date ——
GLORIA. Who asked you? (*Changes tone.*) Any suspicious letters or phone calls from women?
AUDREY. Erwin wasn't like that. He was different!
GLORIA. Different ——
AL. Hey—toots —— (*Shows* GLORIA ERWIN'S *picture as though to prove he wasn't like that.*)
GLORIA. Oh ——

(*Door buzzer.*)

AUDREY. (*Helplessly to* CLARENCE.) If that's the neighbors ——
CLARENCE. Let me —— (*Opens door.* CARVER, *an irascible old gentleman, stands there. He is wearing a worn Prince Albert and striped trousers, black hat.*) Yes?
CARVER. (*Hands* CLARENCE *his hat.*) How do you do? My name is Carver.—WHERE'S ERWIN?
AUDREY. Oh, Mr. Carver, it's so nice of you to come out here. This is my brother, Mr. Dobbins, and this is Miss Gloria Gray of the *Newark Gazette,* and that's—I don't believe I know your—name ——
GLORIA. Just Al, pay no attention to him.
AUDREY. Mr. Carver is my husband's boss.
CARVER. Where's Erwin?
GLORIA. (*Making notes.*) Oh sure—J. G. Carver.—Right?
CARVER. What's the difference? Where is Erwin?—That's the point.
CLARENCE. (*Comes down to him.*) Well, I'll tell you my theory, J. G.
CARVER. Who?
CLARENCE. (*Stops and turns.*) J. G.? Isn't that correct?
CARVER. My name is Carver—call me Carver, Mr. Carver, or Hey You—but don't call me J. G. (*Walks step to* R.)
GLORIA. (*Offering hand.*) My pal.
CARVER. (*Waving it away.*) No. No.—No nonsense.—Where's Erwin?

AUDREY. The detective was here this morning and he said he thought they could trace him. He said lots of men disappear every day—especially married men about Erwin's age.

CARVER. Foolish talk. Foolish talk. (*Crosses below* AUDREY *to* R. *of* CLARENCE.)

AUDREY. He said they generally turned up in hospitals saying they lost their memory ——

CARVER. A lot of pish-posh.—Now here's a man that's a reliable citizen, see—worth more than you or you or any of you—in his way. He's gone!! Where? Nobody knows. It's a silly country. Man phones me, says he's Erwin's manager.—Why don't they trace him? 'Cause they're a lot of fools. Make a lot of mystery out of nothing.—I know where he is.

GLORIA. Where?

CARVER. (*Shakes finger.*) Writing verses for a rival concern.

AUDREY. Oh, but Mister ——

CARVER. (*Upstage and back to* C.) Don't talk. Don't argue. I've figured it out. Thought I didn't appreciate him just 'cause I didn't pat him on the back every minute—along comes some sneak—gives him a lot of sugar and steals him away—no justice anywhere—never was—never will be.

GLORIA. But he'd hardly keep it a secret from his wife.

CARVER. 'Fraid of his wife?

AUDREY. Oh no.

CARVER. Don't argue. Afraid of you. 'Fraid of that man over there —don't know who he is.

CLARENCE. Why, Mr. Carver, I'm ——

CARVER. And I don't care. 'Fraid of everybody—just a poet. Just lives in himself. (*Taps forehead.*) Afraid of me, even. The fact is, that none of you can deny, he's gone—(*Shakes finger.*) and Mother's Day deadline is tomorrow. But I happen to know my rights. I've fought competitors before and I can do it again. (*Phone rings.*) Answer that. And if it's for me, I'm out. (CLARENCE *goes to phone and is seen but not heard talking.* CARVER *to* GLORIA, *then* AL.) Erwin wasn't so good at first. He had the feeling, the warmth and the inspiration to be a top-notch greeting card man, but he didn't have the technique. I taught him all I knew—I worked and struggled to bring him up, up the ladder and then someone steals him from me.

CLARENCE. (*In phone.*) Well, you can if you want to.

AUDREY. Who is it?

CLARENCE. (*In phone.*) Well, we know he took the bus for New York, but go ahead if you want to. (*Hangs up.*)
AUDREY. Who was that?
CLARENCE. The Boy Scouts at Eagleville.
CARVER. What do they want?
CLARENCE. They want to drag the Eagleville Pond for Erwin.
AUDREY. What?
CLARENCE. I told them he wouldn't be there—but they said they'd never dragged a pond before—they wanted to do it anyway.
GLORIA. The Eagleville Pond—where is that?
CLARENCE. It's right down the street.
GLORIA. Come on, Al. We might use that —— (*Starts for door.*)
CLARENCE. It's right next to my property ——
GLORIA. We'll take it anyway.

(GLORIA, CLARENCE *and* AL *go out.*)

AUDREY. I'm sure Erwin wouldn't want to work for anybody but you, Mr. Carver—he was always saying how he liked being in your office and how wonderful you were.
CARVER. I didn't come here to listen to a lot of sentimental nonsense.
AUDREY. No, sir.
CARVER. What I want to know is—did he leave any verses around?
AUDREY. He took them with him ——
CARVER. I mean any old ones? Things he was going to throw away maybe?
AUDREY. He wouldn't let me touch his desk—he was very particular about that.
CARVER. Stuff-stuff-stuff—nonsense—who cares? Did he leave any papers around?
AUDREY. He had a little room way up in the attic where it would be quiet and his desk is all covered with papers ——
CARVER. All right—all right—show me.
AUDREY. But I don't know ——
CARVER. Anything he did while working for me is my property. Go ahead with you. (AUDREY *starts up—he follows.*) Easter—I wouldn't care—got a man who can write good Easter stuff—but Mother's Day is Erwin's speciality—nobody in the office has got his touch —— (*They go out of sight and we hear him continue to grumble as voices grow farther away.*) Printers have to have the proof way in advance—if I'm late then they charge me overtime . . . overtime, double time, all kinds of time . . . bunch of crooks

—can't plan anything—raise prices—pay 'em more every year, get less work every year—the whole country is going to the dogs as fast as it can go.

(Upstairs a door slams, shutting off the then distant voice. ERWIN *enters, followed by* MABEL *and* FRANKIE.*)*

MABEL. This the place?

ERWIN. Dearie.

MABEL. Oh, it's cute.

ERWIN. Dearie.

FRANKIE. Ain't she to home?

ERWIN. *(Sad.)* I guess not.

MABEL. Most likely went to a movie.

ERWIN. Guess so. Thought maybe she'd be worried about me, but ——

FRANKIE. No—no—she wouldn't be worried.

ERWIN. Of course not. Maybe she's upstairs and can't hear me ——

(Starts up.)

FRANKIE. *(Stopping him at foot of stairs.)* No, wait—listen—before you do anything else, you got to phone Patsy.

ERWIN. Well.

FRANKIE. You promised, didn't he, Mabel?

MABEL. Sure you did, Erwin. *(Goes up to door.)*

FRANKIE. What's the matter, Erwin? You got them selections, ain't you?

ERWIN. Yes, I told you I had.—Dearie.

FRANKIE. Well, you're acting kind of funny.

ERWIN. No, I'm not; honest I'm not.

FRANKIE. Where's your phone?

(ERWIN *points.*)

MABEL. *(At door.)* Hey, look—there's a lot of people up there.

FRANKIE. *(Pulling her into room.)* Never mind what anybody's doing—keep working on him, will you?

MABEL. *(Shaking him off.)* Well, Erwin's going to phone.

ERWIN. Sure, I'm going to—I just wonder where my wife is, that's all.

FRANKIE. Well, geez, this phoning is much more important, you know that, Erwin—you can look for your wife later. Shall I call the number for you?

ERWIN. (*Going to phone.*) No. I'll do it. You don't see a note around for me, do you? (FRANKIE *looks.*) You'd think she'd have left a note. (*In phone.*) Hello—I want —— (*Rises.*)

FRANKIE. What's the matter?

MABEL. (*In phone.*) Penn 6–5892 ——

ERWIN. Suppose Audrey's mad! Suppose she's gone back to live with her mother.

FRANKIE. She hasn't. She don't even like her mother—she likes you better—what the hell ——

MABEL. Hello.—Kitty, give me Patsy's room ——

FRANKIE. Look—everything is around here, ain't it? If she'd gone away she'd pack up, wouldn't she? Sure.

MABEL. (*In phone.*) This is me. He's here. Have you got a paper and pencil?

ERWIN. Well, I guess that's right.

FRANKIE. She's just gone out to get a litle fresh air—that's all. You want her to be healthy, don't you?

MABEL. (*Passes phone to* ERWIN.) Here you are. Patsy's waiting.

ERWIN. Hello—yes, this is Erwin.—What? Oh—oh, yes, horses. Just a minute. I've got them —— (*Gets out book to read list.* FRANKIE *pulls paper out of pocket to compare lists.*) For the first race Sunador—second Frolic—third Motto—fourth Mr. Khayyam —— Well, that's all . . . yes, I know, but I didn't figure the rest of them yet . . . I thought I'd get the others on the way back.

FRANKIE. (*To* MABEL—*holding his list.*) I missed every one.

MABEL. What do you mean?

FRANKIE. I thought I'd see if there was anything in this bus business for me, too, maybe—so you know when I went to the rear seat and sat by myself?—I was trying to dope 'em, and I wrote 'em down all right, but I didn't hit a single one. (*Crumples paper and throws it on floor.*) Well, that shows it ain't just the bus anyhow.

ERWIN. Certainly I will—but I have my verses to think of too, you know—and ——

(AUDREY *enters from stairs.*)

FRANKIE. (*Tipping his derby.*) Oh—how are you?

AUDREY. Erwin.

ERWIN. (*Grins.*) Audrey—I was looking for you. I yoohooed a couple of times but —— (*In phone.*) Well, good-bye, I got to talk to my wife. Dearie —— (*Hangs up and rises. Going to her.*) These are my friends.

AUDREY. Oh, Erwin—(*Rushes to his arms.* ERWIN *looks at others pleased.* FRANKIE *gestures I-told-you-so.*) I've worried so—I couldn't imagine —— (*Draws back.*) Where have you been?

ERWIN. Up at the hotel with them—him. Oh, Dearie—I've got so much to tell you ——

FRANKIE. (*Taking* ERWIN *by arm.*) Listen, Erwin—them last two races.

MABEL. Yeah, we better get started.

ERWIN. Oh yes, of course—I can't tell you everything now, because we have to hurry right back again.

AUDREY. Is anything wrong?

ERWIN. No, no, everything's fine. And I'm going to give you a lot of money—over a hundred dollars.

AUDREY. I don't need any money, Erwin.

ERWIN. I'm going to give to you anyhow. (*Searches through clothes.*)

AUDREY. Where'd you get it?

ERWIN. (FRANKIE *starts to drag* ERWIN *out.*) The horses.

AUDREY. Horses?

(CLARENCE *appears in door.*)

ERWIN. Yes. In my little book, you know. It's been quite a source of revenue just for advising.

CLARENCE. (*Coming into room.*) Well, well, well ——

ERWIN. But don't tell him.

CLARENCE. Don't tell me what?

MABEL. I think your house is swell, Mrs. Erwin. I'd just like to own it myself.

FRANKIE. (*Grabs him.*) Say, I don't want to rush you, Erwin, but ——

ERWIN. Yes, we must get started.

CLARENCE. You going away already? Where you been?

AUDREY. Erwin, you'll be back?

ERWIN. Oh sure.

FRANKIE. Sure. He'll be back on the bus—every day—back and forth—you know . . . (*Grabbing him by arm.*)

ERWIN. Audrey.

FRANKIE. Remember your promise, Erwin.

ERWIN. Yes, yes, I know. I know. Oh, wait a minute. (*Breaks aw*[illegible]. *Rushes back to kiss* AUDREY.) See you tomorrow ——

(MABEL, FRANKIE *and* ERWIN *hurry out.*)

CLARENCE. Where's he gone?
AUDREY. (*Calling at window.*) Erwin.
CLARENCE. (*Follows.*) Where'd he get the money? What'd he say? What's he doing? What did he mean—don't tell me?
AUDREY. Oh, dear ——
CLARENCE. Where's he gone? Where's he living? Who are those people with him?
AUDREY. (*Starts.*) He didn't even tell me where he was . . .

(CLARENCE *stops her.*)

CLARENCE. And why did he say "don't tell me"?—What is it he doesn't want me to know? He's got a horse, that's it—and he won't tell me.

(CARVER *enters from above.*)

CARVER. I found a few odds and ends that Erwin had apparently discarded as not good enough—but I think I can use them—I'll have to.
AUDREY. Oh. Mr. Carver—I forgot to tell him ——
CARVER. What do you mean?
AUDREY. Erwin was here—he just left.
CARVER. Where? Where's he gone? (*Rushes out.*)
AUDREY. (*Starts after.*) They went up that way, I think. (*Outside.*)

(CARVER *and* AUDREY *exeunt.* CLARENCE *goes to door, then turns and sees paper left on floor by* FRANKIE. *He picks it up, unfolds and reads, his eyes bulge with excitement.* CARVER *re-enters, followed by* AUDREY.)

CLARENCE. Huh.
CARVER. It's your fault—it's all your fault. You should have called me. No wonder Erwin isn't farther ahead in the world. He's got an incompetent wife—that's what's the matter. You don't know where he is. Let him get away without finding out where he is.
CLARENCE. I know where he is.
CARVER. What? What'd you say?
CLARENCE. He's at the Lavillere Hotel.
CARVER. Where's that? Whoever heard of such a place? What are you talking about? How do you know?
CLARENCE. They dropped this paper.

CARVER. They? Who's they?

CLARENCE. There was a man and woman with him.

CARVER. Oh, so that's it—unscrupulous competitors—trying to ruin my Mother's Day output—I'll show 'em—I can fight for my rights —I'll show 'em—we'll see about that. (*He gets his hat and goes.*)

CLARENCE. He thinks they want Erwin's verses, but I know better. Look —— (*Shows paper.*)

AUDREY. What's that?

CLARENCE. Horses. That's what he didn't want you to tell me, isn't it?

AUDREY. Yes, but ——

CLARENCE. I found this on the floor.—It's their list of the winning horses.—Thought he'd hold out on me, did he—we'll, I'll show him —— (*Stands.*)

AUDREY. What are you going to do?

CLARENCE. (*Gets phone.*) I'm going to bet my shirt.

BLACK-OUT

Orchestra plays "Horses"

ACT III

SCENE 2: *The Hotel Room.*

TIME: *The same afternoon.*

AT RISE: HARRY, MOSES, PATSY, CHARLIE *and a* CHAMBERMAID *are copying verses. The maid is a Swede.* PATSY *is seated at the desk.*

CHARLIE. (*Crossing and looking over* PATSY'S *shoulder.*) I ain't so sure Mr. Carver is going to like your handwriting.

PATSY. What's the matter with it?

CHARLIE. Plenty.

PATSY. To hell with Carver.

CHARLIE. Why don't you do it like her?

PATSY. Aw—she writes like a pansy.

CHARLIE. That's the way you're supposed to write. (*Sarcastic.*) The idea is so that somebody else can read it, see? (*Crosses to* R. *to* MOSES.)

PATSY. The idea is to get 'em done by the time Erwin gets back, that's all.
CHARLIE. Yeah, but we want him to like the job, don't we? We got to keep him contended. My God—look at what Moses is doing—what language you writing that in? African?
PATSY. Who appointed you foreman anyhow? Get busy instead of criticising so much. The thing is to be able to say they are copied.
CHARLIE. (*Sits on bed.*) Get busy yourself, you tore 'em up. I'm tired ——
PATSY. What're you so tired about?
CHARLIE. Do you think it's easy to find a synagogue?
PATSY. (*Suddenly.*) Geez, we forgot all about the second race —— (*In phone.*) Let me talk to Gus. (*Sharply, in phone.*) Well, listen, Kitty, keep this wire open all the time, will you? This is important. To hell with Mr. Shapiro—what is more important—cloaks and suits or horses?—well, I'm tellin' you.
MOSES. Lord and mercy. (MOSES *starts out.*)
PATSY. Where you going?
MOSES. Somebody is pushin' that bell right through the elevator, Mr. Patsy, but I'll be back. (*Gives* CHARLIE *paper.*) I got this one all straight exceptin' one word down there in the corner. (*He exits.*)
HARRY. I got an extra word here. What does he need?
CHARLIE. Something to rhyme with—let me see——(*Reading.*) "We trudged our way on Sundays"—something to rhyme with Sundays.
HARRY. (*Looking at his piece of paper.*) No. The word I have here is "blue-birds."
CHARLIE. The only word I can think of is undies, but I don't suppose Erwin would want to use that.
PATSY. (*In phone.*) How is it, Gus—over? (*Turning to others.*) "Frolic" in the second race.

(*They all cheer.*)

HARRY. Atta baby. (*Jumps up spilling papers.*)
CHARLIE. Hey, look out for them poems.
HARRY. I'm one hundred and four dollars to the good. Yeah ——
PATSY. Pipe down, will you? (*In phone.*) That all goes on "Motto" in the third. Sure, it's a parlay. What the hell do you think—we're pikers? . . . What are you crabbin' about? . . . Well, don't forget you ain't the only bookie. . . . What's the matter? You yellow?

CHARLIE. Come on, Harry, help me pick them up. (*Starts to pick up papers.*)
HARRY. I got to listen.
CHARLIE. Suppose Erwin comes back and finds they ain't ready. He's liable to dry up on us before we get the last races out of him.
HARRY. Geez, that's right. We got to think about the future. (*Stooping to pick up verses.*)
PATSY. (*Back to phone.*) Sure we got a system—but he ain't here now. We sent him out to get some air. . . . How much? (*To others.*) He wants to buy a piece of Erwin.
MAID. What?
PATSY. (*Into phone.*) Never mind how we got him—we own him, that's all. What's your offer for ten per cent? . . . Well, he ain't missed yet, has he? Wait till you pay up on this four horse parlay and you'll think so. . . . We wouldn't even consider an offer like that. (*Hangs up.*) A lousy two grand for ten per cent of Erwin.

(*Crosses over* R. *in disgust.*)

CHARLIE. Maybe we ought to take it.
PATSY. What for?
CHARLIE. (*Goes to* L. *of* PATSY *over* R.) Well, supposing something went wrong?
PATSY. What're you talking about?
CHARLIE. Supposing this guy Erwin's holding out on us.
PATSY. Why you . . .
CHARLIE. Well, look, what does he give us over the phone . . . "Mr. Khayyam" . . . and what does he give us under the pillow . . . "Equipoise."
PATSY. What of it? Maybe that's the way he warms himself up. (*Phone. Crosses below* CHARLIE *and* HARRY *to phone* L.)
HARRY. There's your poetry. Geez, a hundred and four dollars. I think I'll buy Erwin a necktie.
CHARLIE. He's got a necktie.
PATSY. (*In phone.*) Yeah? (*Turns to* HARRY.) It's Mac; he wants you to come right down.
HARRY. Huh. Tell him I took the day off. Tell him I've resigned.
PATSY. He's quit. He's too rich to work.
HARRY. I can't be bothered with that small time stuff . . . all I want is to be able to follow Erwin around for the rest of my life. (*Crosses below* CHARLIE *to dresser* R. *with papers.*)

PATSY. (*In phone.*) . . . and don't keep callin' us up, we want this wire open. (*Hangs up.*)
HARRY. I guess that surprised him, huh? I don't think I was meant to be a barkeep anyway. (*Sits at dresser down* R.)
PATSY. Now to hell with all that. Let's get this stuff copied.
HARRY. Sure. All right. I'm just as anxious as you are. After all I got some rights to Erwin, ain't I? Who discovered him in the first place?

(MOSES *and* CARVER *enter up* L.)

MOSES. (*Enters.*) Yes sir, but I don't know if they . . .
CARVER. (*Enters.*) Never mind about that boy. . . . Who's in charge here?
PATSY. Who are you?
CARVER. My name's J. G. Carver in case you're interested . . . and I'm here to tell you I know my rights.
CHARLIE. I guess you got the wrong room, brother.
CARVER. Don't try to shilly-shally with me. I've had the call traced . . . I know all about what's been going on here from A to Z. You kept him here all right . . .
HARRY. We what?
CARVER. You've been stealing his verses, the very verses he'd been working on under my instructions. I know what you're doing . . . all of you. . . . Yes, and you too. (*To* MAID.)
MAID. (*Rises.*) I tink I better go now.
PATSY. Stay where you are, keep copying.

(MAID *sits.*)

CARVER. You can all hear what I have to say . . . and if I don't get action any other way, the United States court will hear about it, let that be understood . . .
PATSY. What the hell is it you want?
CARVER. I want Erwin Trowbridge.
HARRY. (*Jumps up.*) What?
CHARLIE. (*Pulls him back.*) Take it easy.
CARVER. I want him back in his office by tomorrow morning, or I'll have subpoenas enough flying around here to make your eyes water. (*Phone rings.*) If that's for me, I'm out ——
PATSY. (*At phone.*) Hello.
CARVER. There's no individualism in an organization like this . . . it's a bad thing for him.

PATSY. (CHARLIE *goes over to* R. *of* CARVER.) It's the third race, boys. Bounce him out of here.
CARVER. I ain't afraid of you fellows or any other greeting card company in the United States.
PATSY. Pipe down, will you?
CARVER. (*Struggles.*) I'll fight all of you.
PATSY. Did you hear us? Pipe down. . . . Get him out of here, will you, boys? The bum's rush. Want me to miss this race?

(CHARLIE *and* HARRY *grab him by the seat of his pants, knocking his hat off.* MOSES *picks up hat.*)

CHARLIE. Come on, Bo . . . scram.
HARRY. Leave him to me, I can handle him.
CARVER. Take your hands off me.
MOSES. Here's your hat.
PATSY. (*At phone.*) Coming down the stretch, eh? Who's in the lead?
CARVER. I'll have you blackguards in jail. Every one of you.
HARRY. I've thrown out tougher guys than you.
CHARLIE. Don't hold back . . . I'll give you the boot.
MOSES. Better take your hat.

(CHARLIE, HARRY *and* MOSES *return shutting door.*)

MAID. I've found the last line.
PATSY. (*Rises. In phone.*) "Motto," huh?
HARRY. (*Re-entering.*) He won't be back.
PATSY. "Motto" wins.
HARRY. Motto?
PATSY. We won . . . we won. Hold on a minute, Gus.
HARRY. Motto wins, Charlie.
CHARLIE. He won, huh?

(CARVER *throws open door.*)

CARVER. I've been in business since 1898. (CHARLIE *slams door shut.*)
CHARLIE. Out and stay out.
MAID. (*Giving* PATSY *papers.*) That's the last one. Is there anything else?
PATSY. (*Extracting five dollar bill.*) Yeah. Here's a fin for you. Go downstairs and put it on Mr. Khayyam in the fourth race.

MAID. Please, Mr.—if it's all the same by you—I got a place that's much safer. (*Sticks it down shirt front.*)

(CARVER *at door.*)

CARVER. Don't forget what the code says about unfair competition.
PATSY. Oh, for God's sakes, Harry, take that guy downstairs and throw him in the street. Give him a hand, will you, Moses?

(HARRY *exits.*)

MOSES. Mr. Patsy, I wish you wouldn't mix me up in this thing on account of the race problem.
PATSY. Maybe you're right. (MOSES *and* MAID *exit.* PATSY *back to phone.*) Listen, Gus, it all rides on Mr. Khayyam—the works.—What? . . . All right—then half of it—what do I care?—I'll bet the rest with Eddie. . . . No, I'm not crazy. (*With hand over phone; to* CHARLIE.) Go down and place half the dough with Eddie.
CHARLIE. Let's not bet that half, Patsy, what d'ya say? Equipoise is a pretty good horse.
PATSY. Has Erwin missed yet?
CHARLIE. No-o-o, but ——
PATSY. Then do what I tell you and collect on the straight bets—get going.
CHARLIE. (*Getting coat from head of bed.*) Just the same —— (*Goes to door.*) I'm worried. (*Exit.*)
PATSY. (*Back to phone.*) . . . Yeah, that kind of money don't interest us. Erwin is a gold mine . . . we ain't selling shares for chicken feed . . . all right, all right—you know my number. (*Hangs up.*)

(MABEL *has entered before end of* PATSY'S *speech.*)

MABEL. I seen it, Patsy—I seen it.
PATSY. Seen what?
MABEL. Our little dream house.
PATSY. Oh. Where's Erwin?
MABEL. He's downstairs with Frankie. Oh, Patsy—it's gorgeous—you ought to been there—there was the nicest curtains and little pictures and a real garden and a porch to sit on—and a second floor—only I didn't go up and Erwin says he wants to sell it.
PATSY. (*Crossing* R.) O. K. Buy it. Just don't bother me, that's all.

MABEL. Patsy, don't you think we ought to get married if we're going to live in a house?

PATSY. We'll get married. You can get married any day—(*Going to phone.*) but I got a four-horse parlay on the fire and they don't come up often.

MABEL. They come up too often—they come up and hit you right in the face.

PATSY. What do you mean by that?

MABEL. I think we ought to buy this house before everything goes back into hock.

FRANKIE. What's the matter with the elevator? We had to walk up.

(FRANKIE *enters followed by* ERWIN.)

ERWIN. Are my verses copied?

PATSY. (*Crosses up to* L. *of* ERWIN.) I think you'll find everything in A-1 condition, Erwin.

FRANKIE. Who won the first race?

PATSY. We won the first three. Charlie's out collectin' the straight bets now. We got a parlay—ridin' to Mr. Khayyam.

FRANKIE. (*Sits on end bed.*) Did you hear that, Erwin?—We copped the first three.

ERWIN. (*He is looking at verses.*) What?

FRANKIE. The first three come in.

ERWIN. Oh.

MABEL. I was tellin' Patsy about the house, Erwin; he says we'll buy it. (*She crosses to bureau.*)

ERWIN. (*Looking at verses.*) Gee, I can hardly read these. (*Phone rings.*)

PATSY. (*Answering it.*) Hello—Oh, now you're talkin' turkey, Gus . . . we can close the deal on those terms . . . sure . . . well, Erwin is worth that much . . . he's just like money in the bank. . . . All right—we'll incorporate—but listen, I'm president. (*Hangs up.*) That was Gus. They've come around. I made them guys appreciate Erwin's true value.

FRANKIE. I'll bet we'll make a half million with him.

ERWIN. Oh, this is terrible.

PATSY. What's the trouble?

MABEL. What's the matter, Erwin?

ERWIN. Look at this! (*Crosses to* R. *of* PATSY.)

MABEL. The handwriting?

ERWIN. No. The words. Those aren't my words at all.

(CHARLIE *enters.*)

PATSY. Well?

CHARLIE. I collected the straight bets and the parlay stands. Geez, they certainly are afraid of us—Gus had to lay it off with three bookies.

ERWIN. Oh, Mr. Carver would die if he saw this—I'd lose my job.

MABEL. Looks like one of yours, Charlie.

CHARLIE. (*Going to* ERWIN.) What's the trouble? (*Crosses to* R. *of* ERWIN.)

ERWIN. I couldn't write anything like this ——

CHARLIE. (*Taking paper.*) Write what? Let's see.

ERWIN. It doesn't even scan.

PATSY. (*At desk.*) Well, come on, boys, let's not have any fuss—let's just fix it, that's all.

CHARLIE. I did fix it.

ERWIN. I don't want anything fixed—I just wanted them copied.

CHARLIE. But we lost the last line.

PATSY. What is it? (*Takes verses. Reads.*)

"I wonder if the old church stands
Where we trudged our way on Sundays;
I recall how we sat with folded hands"

ERWIN. That part's all right—see—but the rest of it.

PATSY. "So now I don't ever get drunk no more on Tuesdays or Mondays." (*Looks at* ERWIN.) That's no good, huh?

ERWIN. Oh no—it's awful.

CHARLIE. It's the right idea, ain't it? He's thinkin' of his mother, see ——

ERWIN. No—it's no good ——

FRANKIE. (*Going up to* CHARLIE.) Yeah, you got a crust monkeying with Erwin's verses.

CHARLIE. I was only tryin' to help out ——

PATSY. Well, come on, Erwin—just put in your words. What's the stew about?

ERWIN. I can't think what it was myself now. You got me so upset.

FRANKIE. There, you see—you got him all upset, you mug.

MABEL. What you cheap-skates ought to do is hire some first class poet to write Erwin's verses for him—then he wouldn't have to worry so much.

PATSY. (*Crossing to desk.*) When this four-horse parlay comes in we'll hire Longfellow.

MABEL. You can't hire Longfellow—'cause he's dead—I think he is.

CHARLIE. Here. It all comes to thirty-three hundred dollars. That's on the straight bets. I'm keeping mine. Here's twenty-two hundred. (*Giving* PATSY *roll of bills.*)

PATSY. O. K. Now Erwin gets three hundred and thirty.

ERWIN. I do? All that?

PATSY. That ain't nothin'. Wait till Mr. Khayyam comes through to make that four-horse parlay. (*Pause.*) Here you are, Erwin—three hundred and thirty dollars.

ERWIN. It doesn't seem right.

MABEL. The way you got to figure it out is, Erwin, that we wouldn't have this if it wasn't for you.

PATSY. Well, we might have ——

MABEL. Yeah, we might—but we probably wouldn't. You helped, that's sure.

PATSY. Erwin is always going to get his cut, don't worry. And when this fourth race comes through ——

CHARLIE. *If* this fourth race comes through ——

ERWIN. (*Turns and looks at him.* ERWIN *and* PATSY *look at* CHARLIE, *then at each other.*) Yes. I see what you mean. That's pretty good. (*Laughs.*)

PATSY. (*Alarmed.*) Wait a minute.

ERWIN. (*Sits end of bed. Looking at verses.*) It's funny how one line could get lost that way.

PATSY. Never mind about that poetry for just a minute, will you, Erwin?

ERWIN. (*Absently, pieces of paper in his hand.*) What?

PATSY. Let's just concentrate on this—the fourth race, I mean ——

ERWIN. Of course.

PATSY. We can't lose. Can we, Erwin?

ERWIN. No—I don't think so.

PATSY. Mr. Khayyam is your selection, isn't he?

ERWIN. Oh, yes—that's the horse. (*Sees paper.*) There!—the line —there's the verse.

PATSY. Stop changing the subject.

CHARLIE. Do you think we should shift to Equipoise?

ERWIN. No.

CHARLIE. No. Then why did you write his name on a piece of paper?

ERWIN. I didn't ——

CHARLIE. Oh, you didn't—what about this? (*Flashes paper.*)

ERWIN. (*Takes paper.*) Oh, that?

CHARLIE. Yeah that. Why did you hide it under the pillow?

ERWIN. Oh, that was when I was sitting on the bed trying to dope them and I wasn't sure I could do it—so I wrote Equipoise two or three times just to see how it would look—but I didn't think it looked so good.

PATSY. Oh, you wasn't sure.

ERWIN. No.—Don't you see—I'm surprised at you fellows—you were all right yesterday, when I was sick and you took care of me and all that—but now you're getting greedy.

PATSY. I notice you took your ten per cent all right.

ERWIN. Oh, yes indeed.

PATSY. You wouldn't by any chance be thinkin' about crossin' us, would you, Erwin?

ERWIN. No—of course not.—Oh no ——

PATSY. (*Turning up to* FRANKIE.) All right, boys, everything goes on Mr. Khayyam.

CHARLIE. How much you betting, Erwin?

ERWIN. Oh, I wouldn't bet.

PATSY. (*Coming back slowly to* ERWIN.) What do you mean? Which way wouldn't you bet?

ERWIN. I wouldn't bet on anything. That would spoil it.

MABEL. Sure. Erwin explained that to me.

PATSY. Shut up. (*To* ERWIN.) I thought maybe you ought to bet on this nag, Erwin—you doped him.

ERWIN. But don't you see, if I did ——

PATSY. No, I don't see a thing except that if he's good enough for us to put our shirts on—he's good enough for you too. Just give your bet to Frankie and he'll take it over with him.

(FRANKIE *rises.*)

ERWIN. Well, it'll spoil all my fun—but of course—if you buy the house—then I won't be riding on the bus any more anyway.—Well, I think I'll bet two dollars.

CHARLIE. Two dollars!

PATSY. What are you doing—kidding?

ERWIN. No, I'm serious—I think he'll win. I want to bet two dollars.

PATSY. Well, this is a hell of a joke. We got eleven thousand dol-

lars on Mr. Khayyam and you want to bet a deuce. You can't think much of the horse.

ERWIN. I certainly do—I picked him.

PATSY. Well, then play something worth while.

ERWIN. Oh, I see what you mean. Here, Frankie—put ten dollars on his nose. (*Counts it.*)

PATSY. Frankie didn't hear you.

CHARLIE. No, he's deaf.

FRANKIE. They think you ought to put up some real dough, Erwin.

MABEL. I don't think you ought to make him bet boys.

PATSY. Well, we're going to, whether you think so or not. I wouldn't go so far as to say that Charlie's right about you, but a good-sized bet from you would make me think his heart is in the right place.

ERWIN. All right—here—put a hundred on Mr. Khayyam to show.

PATSY. To show, huh—he's good enough for us to have all we got on his nose and you want to play a lousy century note to show.

(*Knocks* ERWIN'S *arm down.*)

FRANKIE. You better hurry up if you want to get this down.

PATSY. (*Turns to* FRANKIE *on his* L.) Shut up. You're goin' to play what you got—on the nose.

ERWIN. You mean all my ten per cents?

PATSY. All your ten per cents. Hand it over.

ERWIN. (*Hands roll to* PATSY.) Well—all right ——

PATSY. (*Taking bills from* ERWIN'S *vest pocket and adding to roll.*) Here you are, Frankie. (*Gives him money. Goes a step down* L. *to* R. *of* FRANKIE.) Put that on Mr. Khayyam for Erwin—right on the nose.

ERWIN. Hey, wait—my money from the Bowery Savings Bank is in that.

PATSY. The hell with it. If he's good enough for us, he's good enough for you—every nickel. Go on, Frankie.

FRANKIE. O. K. I got to hurry. Excuse me, buddy. (*Goes out.*)

(*When* FRANKIE *opens door to go out we see* CLARENCE *standing in hall. He looks in and sees* ERWIN.)

CLARENCE. (*Pointing.*) There he is. (*Comes in.*) There he is. Hid ing from me, you sneak. You low down cheat. You couldn't come out and fight like a man. You had to trick me—you crook.

PATSY. Hey, wait a minute.

CLARENCE. He pretends he knows all about horse races. He's got a list. He's got a little black book.
PATSY. Yeah—we know all about that.
CLARENCE. He cleaned me out. He tricked me. He left a list on the floor—knew I'd find it ——
ERWIN. That's not the facts at all.
CLARENCE. The double-crossing, Mother's Day crook—I went to the bank—drew all my money out—I'm cleaned—lost every cent.
PATSY. Who is this guy?
ERWIN. He's my brother-in-law.
CLARENCE. Yesterday he had them right—all winners—just to lead me on—(*Harry enters.*) just to make me bet.
PATSY. You're just in time, Harry. Push this guy downstairs, will you?
HARRY. Be glad to oblige, Mr. Patsy. (*To* CLARENCE.) Come on —— (*Takes his arm.*)
CLARENCE. Now just a minute. I don't know who you gentlemen are but I'd like to introduce myself.
HARRY. Tough guy, huh —— (*Grabs him by pants and rushes him out.*)
PATSY. So you'd double-cross your own brother-in-law?
ERWIN. No, I didn't—honestly. He just made a mistake, that was all. I wouldn't cheat anybody —— (*Pause—they look at him.*) You fellows believe me, don't you?
PATSY. (*Drily.*) Sure.
CHARLIE. (*Disregarding* ERWIN.) I told you we shouldn't put everything on Mr. Khayyam —— (*Pause.*) Well, what are we going to do?
PATSY. It's too late to do anything. (*Looks at watch.*) It's post time. I'll go down to Gus's so I can collect as soon as—I mean if Mr. Khayyam comes in. You stay here.
CHARLIE. Don't worry—I'll take care of him. (*Crosses slowly and sits at desk.*)

(PATSY *exits.*)

ERWIN. Gee, you fellows are getting pretty serious. I haven't missed yet, have I?
CHARLIE. (*More to himself.*) Eleven thousand dollars.
ERWIN. Well, I suppose Mr. Carver is waiting for me—I better get my verses together and—get over there ——
CHARLIE. You stay here.

ERWIN. But I can't, I ——

CHARLIE. Until after the race.

ERWIN. But Charlie ——

CHARLIE. (*Makes a gesture of finality and sits by the door.*) After the race.

ERWIN. (*Poetic.*) After the race—(*Sits chair by dresser* R.) after the race —— That ought to lead to something. (*Takes pencil and paper.*)

MABEL. (*Turns on radio.*) Maybe I can get the race on here. (*Goes to radio and turns on wrong stations.*)

ERWIN. W.M.C.A. at the top of the dial—I think.

(MABEL *gets the station.*)

ANNOUNCER. . . . and took the first turn in that order. War Glory, Good Advice, Ladies' Man, and Mr. Khayyam.

CHARLIE. (*At the same time.*) That's it—hold it.

MABEL. (*To* CHARLIE.) Is this our race?

CHARLIE. Yeah—they're on their way.

ANNOUNCER. At the quarter. . . . War Glory, Good Advice, Mr. Khayyam there in that order now. Lady's Man going up . . . yes, past Farino. Good Advice is holding that lead, jockey Meade using his head. There they are at the half, Good Advice, War Glory, Mr. Khayyam. Mr. Khayyam driving now—rushing in there. Ah, there's a tumble, a spill. Chase Me stumbled, throwing the jockey, Slate. But he's all right. Slate's all right. That's the three quarter pole. Mr. Khayyam still leading with Lady's Man coming up and War Glory right behind. There they come fast into the stretch. Looks like a little shoving there . . . no, no, it's all right I guess. At the stretch coming down there with a rush, Eq—Equipoise passes Mr. Khayyam, Sun Archer right behind. Yes,—yes, that's the finish. Equipoise wins. Equipoise, the Whitney horse with Workman up. Mr. Khayyam second and Sun Archer closed fast to get third and in the money. Those who backed Equipoise had something to be thankful for today. (MABEL *turns off radio.*)

ERWIN. Well that's too bad.

CHARLIE. Yes, it's just too bad.

MABEL. Ah, geez, I'm just sick—you know it—I'm just sick to the stomach.

ERWIN. Well, the handicappers were right—they all thought Equipoise would win. Well, that's what makes it interesting.

(FRANKIE *enters.*)

CHARLIE. Where's Patsy?
FRANKIE. He's coming.
CHARLIE. You guys wouldn't listen to me. I been telling you all along—I had a hunch something like this would happen.

(PATSY *enters slowly; comes toward* ERWIN.)

ERWIN. (*Rises.*) I suppose you want your necktie back now.
PATSY. I want more than that.
ERWIN. I feel awfully sorry for you fellows.
PATSY. You better start feeling sorry for yourself.
CHARLIE. He tried to beat it off to the office and leave us holding the bag.
FRANKIE. What his brother-in-law said about him was all true.
CHARLIE. The crook.
MABEL. (*Terrified.*) Boys, what are you going to do?
PATSY. We'll give him something to remember us by. He knew damn well Equipoise was going to win.
ERWIN. I didn't. That's not so.
PATSY. Well, I'll tell you one thing . . . he'll never forget that Mr. Khayyam lost. (*Bing. He hits* ERWIN.)
MABEL. Patsy.
ERWIN. Now wait a minute.
PATSY. Learn you to cross us. (*Grabs him by the coat and hits him again.*)
FRANKIE. Give him one for me.
MABEL. Don't—don't.
ERWIN. Don't you think this is a little drastic?
PATSY. I'll show you what's drastic.
MABEL. Patsy . . . Patsy . . .
PATSY. You keep out of it.
MABEL. Don't hit him again.
PATSY. I ain't started yet. Get a loud station, Frankie. (PATSY *takes off his coat.* FRANKIE *switches on radio.*)
CHARLIE. (*Grabs* MABEL *and holds her.*) Here. Don't try to interfere. That ain't going to do any good.
MABEL. No. . . . No. . . .
PATSY. Listen. I ain't even begun.

(*Radio is heard.*)

CHARLIE. Wait a minute.
ANNOUNCER. Something going on down at the judge's stand and no bets are being paid until the official announcement. Looks like a disqualification to me.
PATSY. What?
CHARLIE. Listen.
ANNOUNCER. Well, well . . . I was all wrong, folks,—I was all wrong. Equipoise did not win after all—the judges have been in a huddle down there at the stand and boy—what excitement—wait a minute, folks,—what is it, Perry? Oh, here's the latest announcement. I just got it—Equipoise disqualified—Mr. Khayyam declared the official winner—Sun Archer second and Lady's Man third. Mr. Khayyam paid 12-1. (FRANKIE *snaps it off.*)

(PATSY *during announcement walks close to the radio. He turns to others with a naive grin.*)

PATSY. We won. (*They look at* ERWIN. PATSY *goes to him apologetically.*) Gee, I'm awfully sorry, Erwin ——
ERWIN. You —— (*Hits* PATSY *a belt in the jaw.*)

(PATSY *staggers back more from surprise than force.*)

PATSY. Hey, what the hell ——
MABEL. You had it coming to you.
CHARLIE. (*Crosses below* ERWIN *to* L. *of* PATSY. *Pushing him about.*) Yeah, I don't blame Erwin. What's the idea of hitting him that way?
ERWIN. Yes, what's the idea? You make me good and mad. (*Takes a swing at* PATSY.)

(PATSY, *mad, would defend himself.*)

CHARLIE. (*Pushing him away.*) Don't hit him, Patsy—he'll quit us.

(CLARENCE *opens* C. *door and comes in. He sees* ERWIN *swinging on* PATSY, *who is apparently afraid of him. He is astounded.* ERWIN *turns and sees* CLARENCE—*full of new-born confidence he rushes at him.* CLARENCE *runs out in fear and slams door.* ERWIN *turns and gets his breath, leaning against door. Hercules has cleaned the Augean Stables.*)

PATSY. (*At desk.*) Come on, Erwin, don't be sore. Announcers don't make mistakes like that often—and geez, we had our shirts up.

AUDREY. (*Enters.*) Thank you very much—Erwin! I want to talk to you.—It's very important. What did you do to Clarence?

ERWIN. Oh, that big ——

AUDREY. Please forgive him—he's lost all his money—he's so upset ——

(CLARENCE *and* CARVER *appear* C.)

ERWIN. Oh, Mr. Carver ——

AUDREY. And, Erwin, will you do me a favor ——?

ERWIN. Oh sure, of course I will, dear ——

AUDREY. Will you speak to Mr. Carver?

ERWIN. Why ——

CARVER. (*Coming* L. *of* ERWIN.) Erwin ——

ERWIN. Yes, Mr. Carver—I'm sorry I ——

CARVER. Have these men a contract with you?

ERWIN. Oh no—no—they just ——

CARVER. Who gave you your start?

ERWIN. You did, Mr. Carver.

CARVER. Who taught you the business?

(HARRY *enters, goes between* CARVER *and* PATSY.)

HARRY. What do I do for the Fifth?

CARVER. Don't interrupt!

HARRY. What do you mean, don't interrupt? (*Slaps* CARVER *on shoulder turning him around.*) Who do you think you are?

ERWIN. Don't talk to Mr. Carver that way.

HARRY. (*Meek.*) Oh, all right, Erwin, if you say so. But what do I do in the Fifth?

PATSY. Shut up.

(MOSES *enters.*)

MOSES. Boy, did I ride home on a cloud of glory!

ERWIN. Get back on your elevator.

MOSES. Oh . . . yes sir, Mr. Erwin.

AUDREY. (*In admiration.*) Erwin.

ERWIN. I'm sorry we've been interrupted, Mr. Carver.

CARVER. I'm going to have the room with the north light repainted and redecorated and you can have that to work in, and I'm going to get you a new desk and put your name on the door and I'll give you sixty dollars a week.

ERWIN. Sixty?

CARVER. Seventy-five dollars. (*Phone rings.*) Don't interrupt, I'm in conference . . . telephones, telephones . . . all day long . . . haven't I had enough trouble . . . I'm sorry, Erwin, I'm sorry.

PATSY. O. K. for me to take that call, Erwin?

ERWIN (*Crosses to* R. *of* PATSY.) Sure, go ahead.

(PATSY *does so.*)

AUDREY. Erwin, please do me a favor . . . go back to Mr. Carver. I know you'll be happier that way.

PATSY. They want to buy twenty per cent of you, Erwin. They've doubled their offer.

ERWIN. Yes. That's all right, except I won't be able to dope them any more.

PATSY. Why not, why won't you?

ERWIN. 'Cause you made me bet.

PATSY. What's the difference?

ERWIN. Well, you can't dope them for money. You just have to do it for fun. I wouldn't have any idea who was going to win now. I told you that. (*Puts hands to his head.*)

AUDREY. (*Crosses below* CARVER *to* R. *of* ERWIN.) What's the matter, Erwin? Do you want Clarence to leave the room?

ERWIN. Mr. Carver, have you got a pencil?

CARVER. (*Hurrying to get it.*) Yes, Erwin, yes, my boy, what is it?

ERWIN. Take this down:

The race is o'er,
We've won, my lad,
Love and kisses
To dear ol' Dad.

(*Raises one finger indicating Father's Day No. 1.*)

CURTAIN

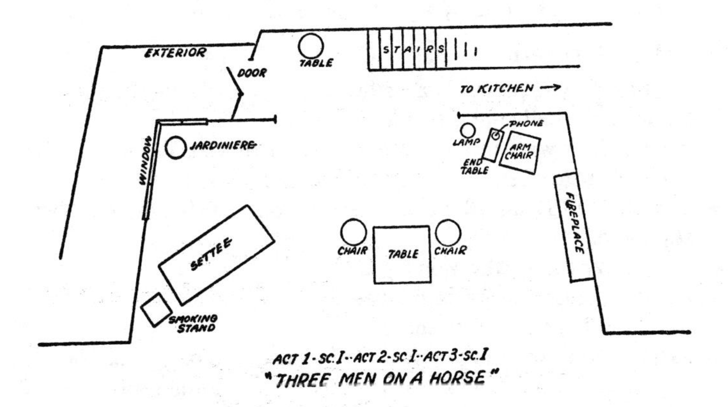

ACT 1 - SC. I - ACT 2 - SC. I - ACT 3 - SC. I
"THREE MEN ON A HORSE"

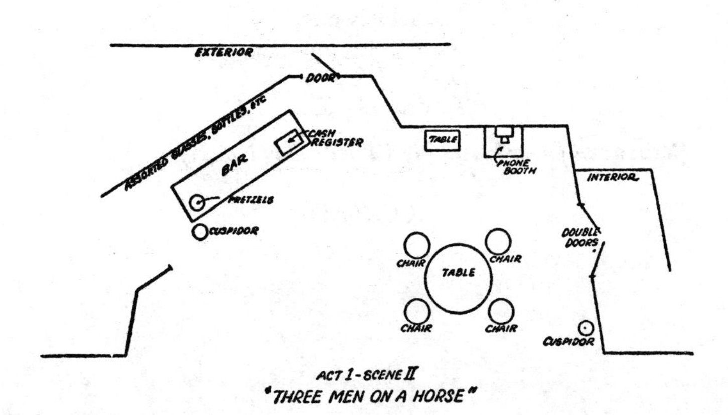

ACT 1 - SCENE II
"THREE MEN ON A HORSE"

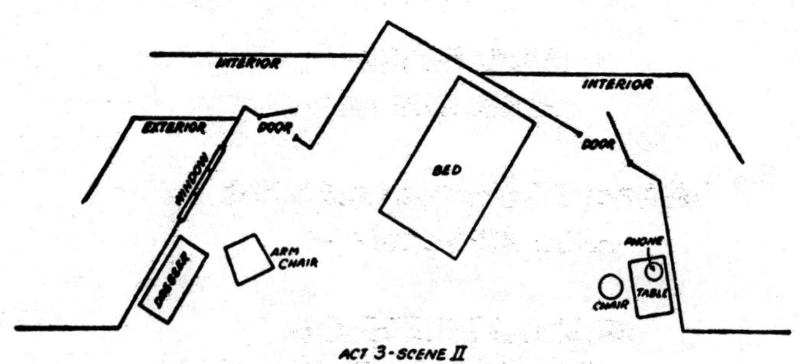

ACT 3-SCENE II
"THREE MEN ON A HORSE"

PROPERTY PLOTS

Act I—Scene 1

Pictures and mirror
1 long rug
1 brownish strip carpet on stairs
1 square rug
1 "Welcome" mat at front door
Light green portieres on window
Glass curtains on window and door
Window shades
Andirons in fireplace
Small stuffed armchair
End table for telephone, date calendar, statuette, N. J. phone book
Stand lamp
Books in niche by pillars
End table, VC doilie, vase and flowers
Small settee with 2 decorated pillows
Smoking cabinet with doilie, account book and box—5 bills inside
Fern and jardiniere
Bridge table
2 straight chairs
- 2 cups and saucers
- 2 teaspoons
- Sugar and cream
- Coffee pot
- Plate of toast
- 2 half grapefruit
- 2 glasses water
- 2 butter spreaders
- Table cloth and napkins

Act I—Scene 2

2 cuspidors
Pictures (wrestlers and race horses)
Round bar table and 4 common chairs
- 2 set ups
- Racing sheets
- Ash tray
- Scratch paper

Practical telephone booth
2 nickels in return slot
U end of bar cash register
Basket pretzels D. end of bar
Assorted bottles on shelves
Assorted glasses on shelves
Towels
Glass water on bar
Box aspirin on shelf
3 cigarettes
Steins
Bottle beer
Ginger ale
Practical bottles
- Beer
- Scotch
- Rye
- Ginger ale
- Tray with pint rye and ginger ale
- (Qt. rye sealed and corked to be wrapped in newspaper)

Act II—Scene 1

Clear bridge table and 1 chair
Set other chair R. of phone table

Act II—Scene 2

Pictures
2 small rugs
Hotel writing desk
- Upright phone
- Phone book
- Dope sheet
- 2 pads, 2 pencils, Hotel stationery } in rack
- Ash tray
- Pad and pencil

¾ bed—made up and spread
- 2 pillows
- Pad and pencil on bed

Light bracket over bed
Light bracket D. R. wall
Glass curtain and portieres
Tapestry over desk
Dresser—runner strip
- Radio
- Tray, pitcher water, 2 glasses
- Neckties, one red, upper D. drawer
- Pad and pencil

Waste basket D. R. of dresser
- Arm chair
  - Plant one verse in it

OFF
- Tomato juice
- 10 verses and corkscrew in bathroom
- Bath towel
- Qt. rye wrapped in a newspaper

Act III—Scene 1

Plant newspapers (*Newark Star*) on settee and armchair L.

OFF
Yellow copy paper—GLORIA
1 sheet hotel paper—FRANKIE
Odds and ends paper—CARVER
Picture of Erwin—AUDREY

Act III—Scene 2

Assorted pads and pencils
Clean up *torn scraps* and plant on foot of bed
Smooth bed
Place broom and dust cloth up stage of hall door.